Awakening Desire

Awakening Desire

Encountering the Divine Feminine
in the Masculine Christian Journey

Irene Alexander

Foreword by Paul Young

CASCADE *Books* · Eugene, Oregon

AWAKENING DESIRE
Encountering the Divine Feminine in the Masculine Christian Journey

Cascade Books
An Imprint of Wipf and Stock Publishers
199 W. 8th Ave., Suite 3
Eugene, OR 97401

www.wipfandstock.com

PAPERBACK ISBN: 978-1-5326-1909-0
HARDCOVER ISBN: 978-1-4982-4517-3
EBOOK ISBN: 978-1-4982-4516-6

Cataloguing-in-Publication data:

Names: Alexander, Irene, author.

Title: Awakening desire : encountering the divine feminine in the masculine Christian journey / Irene Alexander.

Description: Eugene, OR: Cascade Books, 2018 | Includes bibliographical references and index.

Identifiers: ISBN 978-1-5326-1909-0 (paperback) | ISBN 978-1-4982-4517-3 (hardcover) | ISBN 978-1-4982-4516-6 (ebook)

Subjects: LCSH: Christianity—Psychology. | Jung, C. G., 1875–1961

Classification: BR110 .A40 2018 (paperback) | BR110 (ebook)

Manufactured in the U.S.A.   04/13/18

Permission for Hagia Sophia – New Directions Publishing

When he established the heavens I was there . . .
I was beside him like a master builder

LADY WISDOM, PROVERBS 8:27, 30

He was in the beginning with God, all things were made through him.

JOHN 1:2–3

But she is sent in one way that she may be with human beings; she has been sent
in another way that she herself might be a human being.

AUGUSTINE, *ON THE TRINITY*.

Contents

Foreword

To explore the depths of what it means to be human is almost as impossible as to plumb the depths of God. God is a boundless being and although the human being is a creation, she/he is crafted in the image and likeness of God and any boundaries or limitations are set by the infinite God. Because God is an essentially relational being, relationship is both the mystery and crucible of human existence, that which transforms us through the process of community into expanding persons. This is a wonder too beautiful for words, and yet we are compelled rightfully and beautifully to find language to explore what we are seeing. Books, like the one you are holding in your hand, are an integral part of the transition in global community that we are all sensing. To do this, we must integrate both hard and soft sciences, framed by the uniqueness of our own stories. While the melody may be heard in the voice of one, the power of transformation is in the potency of harmony.

There is a significant scene in the novel, *The Shack*, in which Mack encounters God the Father as a black woman. His tortured memories of abuse by his own father, combined with a rigid male-dominated religious tradition, have closed his heart, and when the god of his imagination did not even show up to answer a single question, Mack is furious and rages his disillusionment. Then Papa, a black woman, walks right through his defenses. "For all you have been through, I didn't think you could handle a father right now." The love of God, while respectful of our brokenness and person, is not limited by the imagery with which we have tried to contain God's nature and character. Love works to build bridges into deepening relationship. For many women who have been trafficked by greed and used by sexual domination and objectification, God often comes to them neither as male nor female, but as, for example, a black Labrador Retriever. This is not a God who will take on the persona of our abusers, but will find a way to build even the most tentative bridges of trust, incrementally and tenderly.

Human sexuality is not in essence a conversation about gender and role polarity, nor even about physical and relational interactions. It is a doorway into mystery, the depths of what it means to be human, and therefore also about the essential nature of God. We human beings are created in the image and likeness of God, which at least means this *imago dei* moves in both directions, from and toward our humanity and from and toward God's being. We can work to understand the deepest parts of our humanity, the most authentic longings and aspirations, the innate attraction to integrated living, to peace, kindness, grace and love, to hope and all her children, perceiving the origin of laughter and the love of a parent for a child and in so doing touch the face of God. Likewise, we can see in Jesus, the nature of this God revealed in flesh and blood, in a declaration of our humanity unparalleled and yet visible in each of us, though clouded and covered by the darkness within which we have been long enshrouded.

One of the penultimate wonders which we are invited to explore, is that first declaration about the high order creation that God birthed in to the cosmos. "Let Us create a human being, in our image and likeness. . .in the image of God He created him. . .God created Human in His own image; male/female He created them." Centuries later, Jesus affirms the same declaration in Mark 10:5, "But from the beginning God made them male/female." I have chosen to translate these two statement as male/female, as it is in the original Hebrew and Greek, rather than the common English 'male and female'. In the original, there is no conjunction in either passage, no "and" that suggests a polarity or binary creation. There is within the human creation an essential unity, a continuum that includes the breadth of maternity and paternity, masculinity and femininity, and that spectrum is true of God.

In the darkness of our own independence we have believed massive lies about what it means to be human. Jesus came to expose these lies. The Spirit of God works within us to open our eyes to the truth of what it means to be fully human and fully alive, and to agree with the Truth. Instead of trying to determine and categorize our humanity in binary terms, it is time we open our arms up to the staggering wonder that we have always been a very good creation, lovingly crafted in the image and likeness of God. This book explores the female/male God, a God beyond gender, a God who created the spectrum of gender. God is community. We are part of that community.

FOREWORD

This book invites you to relate to God with all your being, sexual and gendered, and opens the possibility of a fuller understanding of yourself and of God as holistic beings in face to face to face to face relationship.

Paul Young

Acknowledgments

This book has been part of a long slow journey, not the least of which has been my own personal journey engaging with Holy Wisdom. I am very grateful for the guides and encouragers along the ways—spiritual directors, scholars, friends. Particular thanks to the Holy Scribblers, Jill Manton, Charles Ringma, Christopher Brown, and Terry Gatfield.

Special thanks to Karen Wuest-Hollenbeck for her deeply thoughtful, spiritual editing.

And thanks to all those at Wipf and Stock who, through community and commitment, continue to offer support and publication!

Introduction
Mapping the Journey Ahead

He whom neither men nor angels can grasp by knowledge can be embraced by love. For the intellect of both men and angels is too small to comprehend God as he is in himself.[1]

The God of the universe and the Bible is both Mystery beyond our comprehension and One who is closer than breath, self-revealing to those whose hearts are open (Isa 57:15). The fourteenth-century author of *The Cloud of Unknowing* writes that our human minds are too small to understand God. Thus we can only know God as the angels do—through love.[2]

In this book, I hope to awaken our desire to know more intimately the God who breaks through our compartmentalization and naming. In identifying the feminine in God, I am not advocating that we create God in our own image, nor that we change names for God simply because we *want* to do so. Rather, I am seeking to recognize God as Other—One who invites us to relate more deeply and to name more widely, One who seeks to interact with us in order to know us more fully and to love us more truly so that we might know "the breadth and length and height and depth, and to know the love of Christ that surpasses knowledge, so that [we] may be filled with all the fullness of God" (Eph 3:18-19, NRSV).

Growing up in New Zealand in the 1950s, we talked about and prayed to the God of the Bible with strictly masculine language. He was my loving Father God. He was Jesus come to earth to show us what God is like. It

---

1. *The Cloud of Unknowing*, 50.
2. Ibid.

never occurred to me to question this. As a child, I loved Philippians 2, with its description of the God who emptied himself, became a human being, and was willing to die, "even death on a cross" (Phil 2:8, NASB).

By the time I was eight years old, I was reading a chapter of the Bible each day, and my heart was awakened to know God. I identified with the people in the Bible, the families called out of Egypt and led by the Spirit into the Promised Land. I imagined myself as one of the children who were blessed by Jesus, and I longed to be like the disciples who became preachers and teachers around the countries of the Mediterranean. As I read missionary stories and understood that people in India and Africa had other ideas about God, I felt called to be a missionary to lead them to Christ, the true God.

I had no idea that the children growing up in the Promised Land in the biblical period might see God differently from me. For if I had been a child growing up in Israel, I would have experienced the Spirit of God (*ruach*[3]) as female. The *ruach*, the breath of God, brooded over the face of the deep in the creation story and led the people of God into the wilderness, providing them with food and care. In both Hebrew and Aramaic, the word for spirit is feminine. Of course, I would also have heard of God the Almighty, who protected Israel and fought her battles. Yet for the Hebrew people, the God who transcends gender is imaged as a strong tower, a warrior, a shepherd, a kinsman-redeemer, as well as a midwife, a mother bear, and a nesting bird.[4] In recent years, I have begun to discover that the God of the Bible and the early church has been described with both masculine and feminine imagery, referred to by the church fathers and mystics as both Mother and Father.

As I have reflected on the over-masculinized view of God that I imbibed as a child, I have often wondered what it would be like to grow up relating to God with both masculine and feminine language. How would our sense of self and relationships with others be different? Would there be a difference in how we honored and related to the opposite sex? How might our psyches be transformed if we grew up with a God who was not only fighting for us with power, but also gathering us with motherly compassion?

---

3. Theologian R. P. Nettelhorst says that the masculine form of *ruach* is used only nine of the ninety-four times it occurs in the Hebrew Scriptures. All other occurrences are grammatically feminine or indeterminable.

4. These biblical references will be explored in a later section.

If we grow up with an understanding that God is the highest good and the profoundest truth,[5] then we will infer that the highest attributes are those that reflect our understanding of God. In other words, if we believe that God is loving and kind, then we will seek to be loving and kind in the way we live our lives. If we believe that God is patient and compassionate, then we will seek to be patient and compassionate rather than impatient and judgmental. If we believe that God is masculine and not feminine, then (perhaps unconsciously), we will value the masculine and devalue the feminine.

As I came to adulthood in the early seventies, I slowly came to realize that I devalued myself as a woman and did not know why. Even though I knew myself to be loved by a loving father and a loving Father God, there was something in me that valued men more than women—including myself. Similarly, if a young man comes to adulthood relating to God only in masculine terms, he may unconsciously (or consciously) devalue women as well as the feminine within himself. He may esteem the masculine and all that means for him as he finds his place in the world, thus hiding his feminine attributes as unworthy.

When I was in my early thirties, married with young children, I began to realize—as most married people do—that my husband did not fulfill all the needs I had hoped he would. He wasn't quite the knight in shining armor about whom I had dreamed. I had wise mentors, one of whom pointed me towards God as beloved. I meditated slowly through Song of Songs and gradually absorbed the possibility that God looked on me as a lover. I was able to accept that there was no man who would fulfill all my heart's longing because I was made for God. "My lover spoke and said to me, 'Arise my darling, my beautiful one, and come with me'" (Song 2:10, NIV).

I have since asked men about their longing for a lover who can meet all their heart's longing. What do men do when they discover that no human can meet their deepest longing for love, their longing to be known in all of their humanity, including their sexuality? The church fathers and mystics through history have asked the same questions.

In recent years, many books have been written that explore the Divine feminine—some specifically Christian and others from various faith perspectives. My life has led me on a journey of deepening and changing relationship with God through psychology, missions, academia, and spiritual formation. I have written this book with a Christian focus as a complement

5. Johnson, *She Who Is*, 4.

to those already written. In this book, my hope is that regardless of our gender, we will journey towards deeper intimacy with God, who is both father and mother, romantic lover and closest friend. This journey is one of healing and wholeness, which will empower us to bring shalom to our broken world.

MAPPING THE PATH AHEAD

In the following paragraphs, I trace a brief outline of the pathway through this book.

Part I draws on the writings of theologians to explore biblical passages that reveal the presence of feminine images and representations of God in the Scriptures, such as the Spirit, El Shaddai, the Shekinah, Lady Wisdom, as well as the hidden implications of the feminine in the Hebrew and Syriac languages, and the implied (or named) feminine in metaphors of a hovering bird, a midwife, and a mother bear. This opening section also draws from the rich writings of the early church fathers and mystics, which used feminine imagery and names that reveal ancient and traditional perspectives on the Divine feminine. These first four chapters lay the theological, scriptural and historical groundwork so that readers can find their place in the long history of the Christian faith, which clearly names the feminine in God.

In chapter 1, I discuss the power of language to shape our images of God and thus our interactions with God. The Holy Scriptures do not rely on factual, rational, abstract or propositional language, but rather metaphors, analogies, parables, and poetry. Because biblical writings draw images and activate our imagination, they help us in our search for the presence of the Divine feminine.

In chapter 2, I trace an overview of the many scriptural images and metaphors that are either directly feminine or feminine by connotation. We see the more explicit naming of God as female in the Lady Wisdom Scriptures and the El Shaddai verses. The more hidden inferences occur when the Hebrew audience would have heard the feminine in their language; yet without a knowledge of the Hebrew, we have become deaf to the feminine presence in these references. There is also a possibly unnoticed connection between Christ, the Logos of the New Testament, with the feminine Wisdom in the Old Testament.

In chapter 3, I follow this golden thread of the scriptural feminine into the writings from church fathers and the mystics, who give us a window into the use of feminine imagery in earlier times. Various writers in antiquity, who lived nearer to the time of Christ, refer to all three figures of the Trinity with feminine terms, identifying God as feminine. These names are sometimes maternal, but at other times they have erotic or romantic inferences, such as in the personification of abstract virtues, as in Lady Poverty and Lady Compassion.

In chapter 4, I explore how the figure of Mary, the mother of Jesus, is even more personal—a representation of the feminine Divine. As a representation of the Divine, Mary has been elevated to divine/semi-divine status, through whom many receive the nurture of the Divine feminine.

This feminine naming of God was later lost to much of the church—and to the Western world in particular. As our images of God became more exclusively masculine, we separated ourselves from the God who longs to heal us and call us into a balanced masculine-feminine way of being in the world where we are known as the beloved.

In this book, I intentionally draw from the writings of men who have related to the Divine feminine. I know many men who acknowledge the positive contribution of feminist theologians, but some men perceive such writings—along with my explorations in this book—as being 'really for women,' rather than for themselves. Though some may have engaged with the idea intellectually, they may not have been drawn to relate to the feminine Divine in their own spiritual lives.

In part II, I explore the lives of men who have personally encountered the feminine Divine in their own lives and have explicitly engaged female figures to draw us into relationship with the feminine in God. These chapters trace the writings of men from the last two hundred years who wrestle with what it means for us to find the feminine in our relationships with God for spiritual healing, psychological wholeness, and ecological balance. Finding a healthy balance of the feminine within does not emasculate men, but rather invites them towards freedom and fullness of life. Thus these chapters not only explore their ideas, but also the impact of the feminine Divine in their lives.

In chapter 5, I turn to the writings of the Swiss psychoanalyst Carl Jung, who considers the experience of God and the integration of the feminine as essential for wholeness. Though all the other writers in this book are Christian (and Jung did not consider himself an orthodox Christian),

I have drawn on his work because it has been interpreted and applied by many Christian writers. In this chapter, I include discussions of Richard Rohr and James B. Nelson, who use language and conceptualizations that differ from Jung, but who also invite men to unearth and value both the masculine and feminine within.

In chapter 6, I turn to the nineteenth-century novelist George Mac-Donald, who wrote theology as well as fantasy. While MacDonald's favorite name for God in his theological writings is Father of Lights, in his many novels he uses female figures to represent the Divine, such as the North Wind, the great-grandmother, and the Wise Woman. His many stories enable his readers to identify with the masculine journey that seeks both the romantic feminine and the wise woman relationship with the Divine.

In chapter 7, I look at the life and writings of Thomas Merton, a Trappist hermit and activist. Merton's life journey, as revealed in his extensive journals, mirrors some of Jung's analysis regarding the parallel unfolding of the interior and exterior life. Merton's honesty about his own inner journey and his acting out of his deepest desires catapults him towards further wholeness.

In chapter 8, I follow the life of Paul Young, author of *The Shack,* which became a runaway best seller. Young grew up as a missionary kid and then became a successful church worker and businessman; yet he was always hiding a Great Sadness. His representation of God as a black woman opened the possibility of the Divine feminine to millions of people, and his experiential discovery of God's tender mercy touched the hearts of many readers.

In chapter 9, I offer a small sampling of reflections written by men from several different countries about their journey towards discovering the Divine feminine. These responses point towards the ongoing interaction of a God who is living in and engaging our lives and imaginations.

Finally, in the epilogue, I return to the questions I pose here about the difference it might make to our inner souls, our relationships with God, and our relationships with others if we relate to God as both masculine and feminine. My hope is that you may use the writings of these men to reflect on your own experience of God and the feminine and to discover the God of the Bible as the feminine Divine.

1

Talking about God

Language as a Mirror for our Relationship with the Divine

No language about God will ever be fully adequate to the burning mystery which it signifies. But a more inclusive way of speaking can come about that bears the ancient wisdom with a new justice.[1]

Language shapes our perceptions and assumptions about the world, truth, morality, and being. In learning to name, for example, shades of color or varieties of snow, we actually become able to distinguish the differences. More profoundly, the language we use to talk about God shapes our understanding of God and delineates the nature of our relationship with God. Elizabeth Johnson writes about the effects that our images of God have on our values, psyche, behavior, and relationship with the earth. She says that when we talk about God, we give language to what we take "to be the highest good, the profoundest truth, the most appealing beauty."[2] If we talk about God as warlike, someone who smashes his enemies, we as a religious group may in turn exhibit aggressive behavior. If we speak of God as a tyrant, we may disrespect our fellow creatures. But if we describe

1. Johnson, *She Who Is*, 273.
2. Ibid., 4.

God as loving and forgiving, we will care for our neighbors. Our group behavior as well as our individual patterns of life are molded by that which we recognize and name as God. Johnson writes, "God is that on which you lean your heart, that on which your heart depends, 'that to which your heart clings and entrusts itself,' in Martin Luther's memorable phrase . . . the holy mystery of God undergirds and implicitly gives direction to all of a believing person's enterprises, principles, choices, systems of values, and relationships."[3]

If our language about God and our names for God exclude the feminine, then our concepts about God will be proportionately limited by this bias, and we will become alienated from the Divine as well as our neighbors and our inner selves. Johnson explains, "While officially it is rightly and consistently said that God is spirit and so beyond identification with either male or female sex, yet the daily language of preaching, worship, catechesis, and instruction conveys a different message: God is male, or at least more like a man than a woman, or at least more fittingly addressed as male than as female."[4] When we restrict our language for God to the masculine, we will unconsciously value the masculine more highly, and we will give power to the masculine in our social systems and our relationships.

On the other hand, when our language about God includes the feminine—and there are many such instances in the Scriptures—we are invited into a fuller, more liberating and more empowering way of relating to one another and to the God who is beyond our human imagination. For as Johnson suggests, "Language about God in female images not only challenges the literal mindedness that has clung to male images in inherited God-talk . . . such speech calls into question prevailing structures of patriarchy."[5]

Yet we have become accustomed to subtle rules about gendered terms when we speak about God. For example, many people might resist addressing God as mother, even though they would likely accept that God is *like* a mother. When speaking to a crowd of 35,000 at St. Peter's Square on June 7, 2005, Pope Benedict XVI referred to God's maternal love, citing Psalm 111, where God is described as gracious, merciful, faithful, upright, trustworthy. He explained that "'Graciousness' is the divine grace that envelops and transfigures the faithful, while 'mercifulness' is expressed in the Hebrew

3. Ibid.

4. Ibid., 4–5.

5. Ibid., 5–6.

original with a characteristic term evoking the Lord's maternal 'womb,' even more merciful than that of a mother."[6]

The pope is drawing on the Hebrew word *rehem*, which means "womb." The word "compassion" is rooted in the plural form of the same word.[7] Yet in the English translation, we lose the feminine connotation of the Hebrew. In explaining this feminine association, the pope gives permission for his listeners to speak about God using more inclusive terms. Nevertheless, though he says that God's love is *like* maternal love, "the Lord's 'womb'" is not *really* Mother God's womb. In contrast, though we may say that God is *like* a father, we also address God directly as "Father." There is a huge psychological difference between saying God is like a mother and speaking to God *as* Mother. The argument here is that Father is a name for God while feminine images are merely metaphor.

METAPHOR

A metaphor is a figure of speech that uses an image to represent something that is difficult to express in straightforward language. As the fourteenth century author of *The Cloud of Unknowing* expresses it, "He whom neither men nor angels can grasp by knowledge can be embraced by love. For the intellect of both men and angels is too small to comprehend God as he is in himself."[8] Human intellect is too small, for God is mystery beyond our comprehension, and yet God has chosen to reveal God's being to us. Whereas propositional language establishes limits, metaphorical language hints, traces, images, and suggests. As Old Testament scholar John Goldingay expresses it, metaphor and symbol are "intuitive, experiential, self-involving, allusive, plurivocal, holistic, open-ended, dynamic."[9]

In "Female Imagery for the Divine: The Holy Spirit, the Odes of Solomon, and Early Syriac Tradition," Susan Harvey observes that "Metaphor has been the basis of religious language for Christianity from its earliest theological writings, the Scriptures, precisely because of metaphor's capacity to open realms of meaning."[10] Similarly, Richard Rohr says, "Metaphor

---

6. Benedict, "Pope reflects on God's maternal love," lines 14–17.
7. This is further explored in chapter 2.
8. *The Cloud of Unknowing*, 50.
9. Goldingay, *Key Questions about Biblical Interpretation*, 11.
10. Harvey, "Female Imagery for the Divine," 111–39.

is the only possible language available to religion because it alone is honest about Mystery."[11]

Metaphors for God abound throughout the scriptures. As Old Testament scholar Walter Brueggemann explains, "Because humankind is an image, a modeling, an analogy of God, sexual metaphors are useful for speaking of the mystery of God."[12] God is described as a king, a potter, a rock, a tower, a warrior, a midwife, a mother in labor, a shepherd, a father, a lover, the morning star, the sun of righteousness, and many more. Jesus also used metaphors and word pictures to describe himself as the Way, a vine, a shepherd, a bridegroom, and also to describe the kingdom of heaven as a mustard seed, a vine dresser, a sower, a treasure hidden in a field, and a pearl of great price.

Because we cannot know God directly, we need to use word pictures to help us feel after and find God.[13] The images and metaphors awaken within us deeper longings to reach out to God, suggesting the nature of God through word pictures rather than limiting God with strict conceptual language. "When used in religious language, metaphor functions as a verbal icon . . . Thus a religious metaphor is meaningful to the extent that it is grounded in its divine prototype, but by its nature it cannot reduce the divine to a simple definition or identity."[14] Metaphors and images also help us communicate our inner longings and our understanding about God with one another. For recent studies in neurology suggest that metaphors facilitate the emergence of language.[15]

Sallie McFague points out that theology elaborates key metaphors and models about God to evoke understanding that is limited by our ignorance. She warns that "we should not camouflage our ignorance by either petrifying our metaphors or forgetting that our concepts derive from metaphors . . . So we try our different models and metaphors in an attempt to talk

---

11. Rohr, *Immortal Diamond,* 67.

12. Brueggemann, *Genesis,* 33.

13. ". . . that they should seek God, in the hope that they might feel after him and find him" (Acts 17:27 RSV).

14. Harvey, "Female Imagery for the Divine," 111–139.

15. "Our studies of the neurobiological basis of synesthesia suggests (sic) that a faculty for metaphor—for seeing deep links between superficially dissimilar and unrelated things—provide a key seed for the eventual emergence of language" (Ramachandran and Hubbard, "Hearing Colors, Tasting Shapes," 42–50).

about what we do not know how to talk about: the relationship between God and the world."[16]

As observed in the example from the pope's message, some argue that the feminine images of God in the Bible are merely metaphors, whereas the masculine naming of God as Father is a name rather than a metaphor. Yet the biblical narrative and ancient Christian writings reflect a complex interplay of feminine and masculine imagery. The Syriac language, which was used in the first few centuries AD, was very similar to Aramaic, the language used by Jesus and the disciples, and so it can provide clues to early Christian thought. In Harvey's exploration of the Syriac language, "the imagery tells both who humanity is (male and female, in the image of God), and who God is (more than gender can convey). At the same time, it bears witness to the notion that gender—but not one gender only—is somehow fundamental to both human and divine identity, albeit in ways that do not fit the human social conception (or construction) thereof. Gendered imagery here has its basis in the Godhead, not in the human biological or social order."[17] She also points out that the Spirit is specifically designated as feminine.

Ephrem, the fourth-century poet and theologian, delights in the many metaphors for God, noting that they keep us from seeing God too narrowly. He writes, "In his love He made for Himself a countenance so that His servants might behold Him; but, lest we be harmed by imagining He was really like this, He moved from one likeness to another to teach us that He has no likeness. Blessed is He who has appeared to our human race under so many metaphors."[18]

IMAGINATION

Ephrem describes our need for metaphors and images of God to help us feel after and find God. Our human capacity to imagine allows us to picture God through images and to experience God as a personal being with whom we can form a relationship. Because we are gendered beings, we imagine God anthropomorphically, with gendered images—a king, a shepherd, a potter. Though some of our images may be without gender, if all of our

16. McFague, *Models of God*, xii.

17. Harvey, "Female Imagery for the Divine," 132.

18. Ibid., 138.

gendered images are masculine, we will distort the fullness of who God is, and this will distort our own personhood.

Our images of God are formed from our sociocultural world as well as our primary relationships. They are not "imaginary," as in unreal or made up, but rather vehicles that connect us to God, whom we cannot engage directly through our senses. Many people have sought to understand God rationally through the words of Scripture because they do not trust their imaginations. But throughout the Old and New Testaments, the people of Israel spoke about God in images, using their imaginations to describe their relationships with God.

Yet as Jesus makes clear in his teachings about the Kingdom, our imaginations can also form faulty pictures of God, for many of the parables imply that God is "like this," but not "like that." When Jesus laments that the "people's heart has grown dull, and their ears are heavy of hearing, and their eyes they have closed, lest they should perceive with their eyes, and hear with their ears, and understand with their heart, and turn for me to heal them" (Matt 13:15, RSV), he is longing to transform how people see God—and therefore how they relate to God.

In *The Birth of the Living God*, Ana-Maria Rizzuto, a professor of psychiatry, claims that our images of God are primarily experiential. Those who attend church may be able to describe the theoretical "God concepts" that they have been taught, but most likely these are very different from their *image* of God—their relational and experiential knowing. By interviewing adults about the images of God that have shaped them, Rizzuto confirms that our images of God are deeply rooted in our childhood experiences, particularly our relationships with our parents, which might include an imaginative wished-for parent or a feared parent. The teaching of these images is a delicate process that "demands exquisite attention to the experience of the [person]."[19]

Our journey into a fuller relationship with God will lead us, as Ephrem writes, into new encounters with the One "who has appeared to our human race under so many metaphors." This multiplicity of metaphors saves us from prioritizing one metaphor over another. "Since many of the Old Testament God-metaphors, such as warlord and king were patriarchal the metaphorical fatherhood of God was not only literalized but patriarchalized."[20] The prioritizing of the king metaphor taught humans that God was like

19. Rizzuto, *The Birth of the Living God*, 211.

20. Ibid., 29.

a king, while at the same time echoing back the message that kings were divine and patriarchy was God-ordained.

Yet a close examination of the Old Testament images of God reveals that the Father God is not a warlord king "dominating people or exercising coercive power over them."[21] For example, in the book of Hosea, God is depicted as a husband who will not divorce his unfaithful wife, Israel, in the same way that Hosea does not divorce his adulterous wife. Similarly, Jesus sought to change people's perceptions of God by telling stories that conveyed transformed images and representations of God. For example, in the parable of the prodigal son, Jesus paints a picture of a father loving us beyond our childhood fears of a demanding and unforgiving God. Moreover, because "Jesus experienced God as an intimate and tender parent, not as a powerful patriarch,"[22] he heals the image of Father God when he refers to God with the intimate expression, Abba—Daddy.

In *Women and the Word*, Sandra Schneiders writes about this need to heal our images of God: "just as the self and world images can be healed, so can the God-image. It cannot be healed, however, by rational intervention alone . . . a healing of the imagination which will allow us not only to think differently about God but to experience God differently . . . What must be undertaken is a therapy of the religious imagination."[23] Schneiders names our need to widen our metaphorical language for God in order to engage the feminine. She notes the wounding that men may experience in their relationships with their mothers:

> . . . men often fail to negotiate that passage to adulthood which consists in coming to terms with the mother who remains an ever-numinous presence threatening the male with dark possibilities. Although for different reasons, both women and men need to encounter the feminine God. Only a healing of the patriarchal imagination can make this possible . . . Important as correct ideas of God may be, it is the imagination which governs our experience of God because it is the imagination which creates our God-image and our self-image. Consequently . . . the imagination must be healed.[24]

21. Ibid., 30.

22. Ibid., 44.

23. Schneiders, *Women and the Word*, 19.

24. Ibid., 69–71.

SUBJECTIVE IMAGES

In the introduction, I recount my personal experience of growing up in the Christian faith and only speaking about a male God. Many of us have developed confining childhood images of God that influence us into adulthood, since these subjective imaginings are the building blocks for our ongoing relationship with God. Yet if these early imaginings are inaccurate, how can they be transformed?

The psychiatrist and author Scott Peck recognizes the importance of our spiritual journeys. In *People of the Lie*, Peck admits that his subjective images of God are male: "God is not neuter. He is exploding with life and love—even sexuality of a sort. So 'It' is not appropriate. Certainly I consider God androgynous. He is gentle and tender and maternal as any woman could ever be. Nonetheless, culturally determined though it may be, I subjectively experience His reality as more masculine than feminine."[25]

In English, we necessarily use the gendered pronouns "he" and "she." As Peck points out, referring to God as "It" does not represent God accurately as One who is personal and full of life. Some people try to solve the issue of male names or pronouns by using non-gendered words—Parent instead of Father, Creator instead of Mother, but this also signifies God as less personal, more distant. The alternative that I am following in this book is to continue to use the gendered words, such as Father and Abba, but also to use Mother and the pronoun "she." In *She Who Is*, Elizabeth Johnson concludes that the "I am who I am" of Exodus 3 can be understood, with both theological legitimacy as well as religious and existential necessity, as "She Who Is."[26]

As you read this book, my hope is that you will become more conscious of your subjective images of God so that you can bring them into God's presence to be enlivened, healed, and transformed.

READING THE SCRIPTURES FROM A PERSONAL STANCE

When I started studying psychology in the 1970s we were told we should leave our values and religion at the door of the counseling room. Now counselors and psychologists are encouraged to include spirituality in their counseling, and to name their values honestly. It is recognized in a

25. Peck, *People of the Lie*, 12.
26. Johnson, *She Who Is*, 243.

post-modern world that we come to all encounters—whether with text, or in our relationships, or with God—with our own subjective perspectives, assumptions and agenda, and it is more honest to state these up-front.

Similarly theologians now recognize that it is not possible to come entirely objectively to the Scriptures. While the biblical narrative of our covenant-keeping God is clear, there are many smaller points about which we cannot state with certainty and total confidence "The Bible says." A premodern reading of the Bible accepted its contents literally. A modern reading tried to interpret what the writer was hoping to communicate, and therefore analyzed sociological and historical context. In a postmodern world the possibility of this approach is questioned. In a word, as Old Testament scholar, John Goldingay says: "We are critical about what anyone says the Bible says,"[27] being aware that even the university and the church are fallible in their interpretations.

Certain theological approaches have taught us the richness of diverse interpretations. For example liberation theology has come to the scriptures with a specific enquiry about how the marginalized are to hear and respond to a God who cares for the oppressed, and feminist theology has asked the question whether women may recognize differences in the narratives to which men are blind. These are examples of "reader-response" approaches: "readers with particular backgrounds are able to perceive, articulate, and respond to aspects of the texts which readers with other backgrounds may miss."[28]

In writing this book I have come to the text with a particular question about how I, as a child of the twentieth century, pictured and related to God. I have asked whether a child growing up in Old Testament times hearing the original languages may therefore have pictured God differently. Or a person in New Testament times hearing the words of Jesus or the discussions about the Holy Spirit, may have caught resonances of the Divine Feminine, denied to our ears. My purpose in exploring the Scripture passages is to peel back some of the layers and expose the possible meanings and whisperings of the God who calls our hearts to deep healing and intimacy.

The following chapters focus on images of God in the Scriptures, the writings of the early church fathers and mystics, as well as contemporary authors. May these images awaken our imaginations and beckon us into a

---

27. Goldingay, *Key Questions*, 44.

28. Goldingay, *Approaches to Old Testament Interpretation*, 197.

deepening and widening relationship with God, who is our lover, mother, father, and much more.

2

The Ground on which We Stand
Biblical Images of the Feminine

When Israel was a youth I loved him, and out of Egypt I called My son.
The more they called them, the more they went from them;
They kept sacrificing to the Baals and burning incense to idols.
Yet it is I who taught Ephraim to walk, I took them in My arms;
But they did not know that I healed them.
I led them with cords of a man, with bonds of love,
And I became to them as one who lifts the yoke from their jaws;
And I bent down and fed them. (Hos 11:1–4)

IMAGES OF GOD

In the previous chapter, I note the fact that some theologians (including the pope) differentiate between the names we use to address God and metaphors we use to talk about God. In this chapter, we will look for these subtle differences within the biblical images of God. We will consider whether the Bible speaks to God only in masculine terms and whether or not feminine images are used strictly as metaphors—for example, to say that God is *like* a mother without ever addressing God as Mother.

In fact, the Old Testament rarely refers to God as Father, although the masculine form of address became more common during the time of Jesus.[1] Old Testament scholar Tim Bulkeley suggests that the sparing use of the terms mother and father may have been to differentiate the God of the Israelites from the gods of the surrounding cultures. "The gods and goddesses of Canaan, and of every other ancient Near Eastern culture except that portrayed in the ideology of the Bible, were imaged by statues based on human and animal forms. Such 'gods' could easily be thought of as gendered. Indeed, to avoid such implication is difficult, for the image almost has to be either male or female. Only the Bible's aniconic God could avoid being of one sex or the other."[2] Bulkeley uses the term aniconic to refer to *word* pictures (as opposed to iconic, which means using pictures, icons or statues).

In both the Old and New Testaments, such metaphors (or word pictures) for God abound. It seems that the prohibition of concrete images does not forbid mental images, but rather rejects concrete images because they might limit our thinking about God. Without metaphors and images, we would think of God as an amorphous mass, a force, an impersonal energy. Yet if we are to live in relationship with God—as both Yahweh and Jesus invite us to do throughout the Scriptures—we need to be able to imagine God through word pictures and metaphors—in human, animal, and anthropomorphic forms (the lion, the lamb, dwelling under the Almighty's wings, a hen gathering her chicks, a dove). Thus images are not wrong, but they are limited. For if I only think of God as the Lion of Judah, I will fail to see God as the Lamb. If I only see God as the parent of a small child, I will miss seeing God as one who calls me to adulthood. If I only see God as male, I will miss seeing her as female.

As theologian Sallie McFague points out, we are seeking to see and understand the invisible God through the many word pictures scattered throughout the Bible. She cautions, "What this sort of enterprise makes very clear is that theology is *mostly* fiction: it is the elaboration of key metaphors and models. It insists that we do not know very much and that we should not camouflage our ignorance . . . forgetting that our concepts derive from metaphors."[3]

---

1. Bulkeley, "The Image of the Invisible God," 34.
2. Ibid., 22.
3. McFague, *Models of God,* xi–xii.

PARENTAL IMAGERY

The verses from Hosea 11 quoted at the beginning of the chapter are often interpreted as a father speaking, but the imagery is parental rather than masculine. As Bulkeley points out, "Interestingly, undetermined parental imagery (as in Hos 11:1ff which mentions parental care rather than naming either parent), and imagery which mentions and so balances both parents (as in Job 38:28f;[4] cf. Jer 2:27[5]) is found . . . At times the writers seem deliberately to balance motherly and fatherly pictures."[6]

There are many examples of metaphors that could be either male or female, but if our perspective has been framed by a masculine God, we will only "see" a masculine picture. Moreover, as Christians, we read the Old Testament with New Testament eyes. Because Jesus introduced us to Abba Father, we see the presence of the Father in the Old Testament images of God, even though parental language (rather than father-language) is used much more often. That understanding of Father God can also be made patriarchal because of the other metaphors of warrior and king.[7] Thus we read the fatherhood of God back into the Old Testament, missing the originality of Jesus' intimacy with Abba—who is both mother and father.

FATHER IMAGERY

Bulkeley observes, "The Old Testament is very sparing in its use of father imagery to speak of God. It prefers language like shepherd, kinsman-redeemer, rock, and other pictures which had less dangerous echoes in polytheistic systems of thought."[8] We see one example where father is implied (although not actually named) in Deuteronomy 1:31: "in the wilderness

---

4. "Has the rain a father [ab]? Or who has begotten the drops of dew? From whose womb [beten] has come the ice? And the frost of heaven, who has given it birth?"

5. "Who say to a tree, 'You are my father,' And to a stone, 'You gave me birth.'"

6. Bulkeley, "The Image of the Invisible God," 33.

7. Schneiders, *Women and the Word,* 29. "Since many of the OT God-metaphors such as warlord and king were patriarchal the metaphorical fatherhood of God was not only literalized but patriarchalized. As both theologian Sallie McFague and biblical scholar Johanna Bos have pointed out, the literalized father metaphor for God has not only died but, in its ascription of maleness to God, it has become actually idolatrous. We have created a false god and substituted "him" for the true God of Judaeo-Christian revelation."

8. Bulkeley, "The Image of the Invisible God," 32–33.

where you saw how the Lord your God carried you, just as a man[9] carries his son, in all the way which you have walked until you came to this place."

Moreover, God is never *named* as father in the Old Testament. Sandra Schneiders points out that "God is actually referred to as father only twelve times in the Hebrew Scriptures and never in direct address."[10] Thus Father is not a name for God, but "a pointer to the free presence of God, which cannot be encapsulated in, or manipulated by names."[11] Five of the twelve references are about the special relationship God has to the king (David and Solomon),[12] the other seven[13] are all in the context of Israel's sin, demonstrating God's endless forgiveness. In none of these references is God acting as a dominating patriarch. Rather, God is depicted more as the father in the prodigal son parable—as paternal rather than patriarchal.

The familiarity we experience with the naming of God as Father is only because we know God as Father so clearly through the New Testament, not the Old. This familiarity would not have been the experience of Mary and Joseph. When they were looking for the twelve year old Jesus they "did not understand the saying which he spoke to them" when he said, "Did you not know that I must be in my Father's house?"(Luke 2:49–50). While there is profound depth to what Jesus is conveying here, this naming of God as Father is not commonplace for them, as it is for us.

9. Man = *ish*.

10. Schneiders, *Women and the Word,* 29.

11. Bos, "When You Pray Our Father," 12.

12. 2 Sam 7:14 ("I will be a father to him and he will be a son to Me"); 1 Chr 17:13 ("I will be his father and he shall be My son"); 1 Chr 22: 10 ("and he shall be My son and I will be his father"); 1 Chr 28:6 ("I have chosen him to be a son to Me, and I will be a father to him"); Ps 89:26 ("I have chosen him to be a son to Me, and I will be a father to him").

13. Deut 32:6, ("Do you thus repay the Lord, O foolish and unwise people?"), Deut 32:18("You neglected the Rock who begot you, And forgot the God who gave you birth. Is not He your Father who has bought you?"); Ps 103:13 ("Just as a father has compassion on his children, so the Lord has compassion on those who fear Him"); Isa 63:16 ("For You are our Father, though Abraham does not know us, and Israel does not recognize us. You, O Lord, are our Father, Our Redeemer from of old is Your name"); Jer 3:4 ("Have you not just now called to Me, 'My Father, You are the friend of my youth?"); Jer 31:9b ("For I am a father to Israel, and Ephraim is My firstborn"); Mal 1:6 ("A son honors his father, and a servant his master. Then if I am a father, where is My honor? And if I am a master, where is My respect?' says the Lord of hosts to you").

MOTHER IMAGERY

Though Old Testament depictions of God are most often parental, there are several passages in Isaiah that depict God with motherly images. These examples from Isaiah show a God who is pregnant (Isa 44:2),[14] in labor (Isa 42:14),[15] nursing a child (Isa 49:15),[16] and offering maternal comfort (Isa 66:13).[17] Clearly, God is content to identify with these unique experiences of womanhood.

Yet the feminine images of God as mother are not all focused on maternal compassion and care. Hosea 13:8 depicts a fierce mother God protecting her young: "I will encounter them like a bear robbed of her cubs, And I will tear open their chests; There I will also devour them like a lioness, as a wild beast would tear them" (NASB).

The image of a mother bird hovering over her young or covering them with her wings appears often in both the Old and New Testaments. Old Testament scholar John Goldingay lists the psalms[18] where we read of "the wings of a mother bird sheltering a baby bird."[19] In Isaiah 31:5, also, Yahweh Sabaoth will shield and protect Jerusalem "Like mother birds hovering over their young,"[20] as Stramara translates it. The Hebrew word for hovering (*rahaf*) is also used in the second verse of Genesis when the Spirit hovers over creation. The action of hovering like a mother bird is "behind the Syriac image of the feminine Holy Spirit."[21] Because *rahaf* has a feminine ending, Stramara has more accurately translated the Hebrew as "mother bird." Similarly, in Matthew 23:37, Jesus uses the metaphor of a mother hen to describe God's longing "to gather your children together, the way a hen gathers her chicks under her wings." This picture suggests that the

14. "Thus says the Lord who made you and formed you from the womb." See also Isa 43:1 ("thus says the Lord, your Creator, O Jacob, And He who formed you, O Israel"); Isa 44:21 ("I have formed you, you are My servant, O Israel, you will not be forgotten by Me"); Isa 44:24 ("Thus says the Lord, your Redeemer, and the one who formed you from the womb, "I, the Lord, am the maker of all things"").

15. "I have kept silent for a long time, I have kept still and restrained Myself. Now like a woman in labor I will groan, I will both gasp and pant."

16. "Can a woman forget her nursing child, and have no compassion on the son of her womb? Even these may forget, but I will not forget you."

17. "As one whom his mother comforts, so I will comfort you."

18. Pss 17;8, 36:7, 57:1, 63:7

19. Goldingay, *Psalms*, 599.

20. Stramara, *Praying*, 90.

21. Harvey, "Female Imagery for the Divine," 116.

image of God's protective wings throughout the Old Testament could be the wings of a mother bird,[22] and indeed his listeners would have heard that resonance.

FEMININE IMAGERY

Some of the feminine associations in Scripture are difficult to recognize in the English translations. As noted in chapter 1, the word for compassion comes from the same root as the word for womb. "In its singular form the noun *rehem* means "womb" or "uterus." In the plural, *rahamim*, this concrete meaning expands to the abstractions of compassion, mercy, and love."[23] For example, the NASB translates Isaiah 49:13 as follows: "For the Lord has comforted His people and will have compassion on His afflicted." Yet Stramara suggests that a closer translation for this passage would be: "For Yahweh comforts his people and displays maternal compassion on his afflicted ones."[24] Similarly, the NASB translates Isaiah 63:15 as: "Look down from heaven and see from Your holy and glorious habitation; Where are Your zeal and Your mighty deeds? The stirrings of your heart and your compassion are restrained toward me." Yet Trible notes that in the final line, "the entire phrase can appropriately be read, 'the trembling of thy womb and thy compassion.'"[25] As Johnson clarifies, "Accordingly, when God is spoken of as merciful, the semantic tenor of the word indicates that the womb is trembling, yearning for the child, grieved at the pain. What is being showered upon the wayward is God's womb-love, divine love for the child of God's womb: 'I will truly show motherly-compassion upon him' (Jer 31:20)."[26]

We see a further example of the nuanced feminine language in Jerome's Latin (Vulgate) translation, which has been lost in English translations. The NASB translates Isaiah 46:3 as follows: "Listen to Me, O house of Jacob, And all the remnant of the house of Israel, You who have been

---

22. For example, see Ps 36:7 ("How precious is Your lovingkindness, O God! And the children of men take refuge in the shadow of Your wings") and Ps 91:1 ("He who dwells in the shelter of the Most High Will abide in the shadow of the Almighty [El Shaddai] . . . He will cover you with His pinions, And under His wings you may seek refuge").

23. Trible, *God and the Rhetoric of Sexuality*, 53.

24. Stramara, *Praying*, 90.

25. Trible, *God and the Rhetoric of Sexuality*, 53.

26. Johnson, *She Who Is*, 101.

borne by Me from birth and have been carried from the womb." Whereas Jerome's Latin translation reads: "Listen to me, O house of Jacob, And all the remnant of the house of Israel, You who are carried by my uterus [*meo utero*], You who are borne by my womb [*meo vulva*]."[27]

The feminine images used for God in the Old Testament include a seamstress (Gen 3:21); possessing a womb (Jer 31:20, Isa 46:3–4); a woman in labour (Deut 32:18, Isa 42:14, John 3:3–7); a nursing mother (Isa 49:15, Num 11:11–14); a mother with her weaned or sated child (Ps 131:1–2); a comforting mother (Isa 66:11–12, Hos 11:1–4, 8–9); a mother bear (Hos 13:6–8); and a midwife (Ps 22:9).

WISDOM IMAGERY

In the opening chapters of Proverbs, Lady Wisdom cries out in the streets, offering wise words at the city gates,[28] warning the young of the dangers of foolish living and inviting all to learn her ways.[29] In chapter 8, she reveals more about who she is: "From everlasting I was established, from the beginning, from the earliest times of the earth . . . Then I was beside Him, as a master workman; and I was daily His delight, rejoicing always before Him, rejoicing in the world, His earth, and having my delight in the sons of men. Now therefore, O sons, listen to me, for blessed are they who keep my ways . . . For he who finds me finds life and obtains favor from the Lord" (vv. 23, 30–32, 35).

Old Testament scholar John Goldingay calls Lady Wisdom "Ms Insight," and explains that the Old Testament "can picture aspects of the one God as distinguishable from God's own being, so that they almost seem to exist in their own right. . .'Ms Insight' is a personification of such an aspect of God rather than a separate person. But the image does suggest that God was not austerely alone while forming the world. Ms Insight stood by Yhwh's side."[30]

---

27. Stramara, *Praying*, 7.

28. "Turn to my reproof, behold, I will pour out my spirit on you" (Prov 1:23).

29. "My son, if you will receive my words and treasure my commandments within you . . . if you seek her as silver and search for her as for hidden treasures . . . then you will discern righteousness and justice and equity and every good course. For wisdom will enter your heart and knowledge will be pleasant to your soul" (Prov 2:1, 4, 9–10).

30. Goldingay, *Old Testament Theology*, 46.

Some scholars argue that the Christ of the New Testament, "in whom are hidden all the treasures of wisdom and knowledge" (Col 2:3), might also be Lady Wisdom in the Old Testament. John Goldingay states "Paul had already seen Christ, God's Son, as the embodiment of God's Insight."[31] A number of early church fathers also proposed this interpretation, including Origen (d. AD 254), who writes: "We believe that the very Logos of the Father, the Wisdom of God Himself, was enclosed within the limits of that man who appeared in Judea; nay more, that God's Wisdom entered a woman's womb, was born as an infant, and wailed like crying children."[32] Similarly, Augustine writes of Wisdom, "But she is sent in one way that she may be with human beings; she has been sent in another way that she herself might be a human being."[33]

Jean Vanier also draws parallels between Wisdom (or Sophia in the Greek) and the Word, the Logos, of the New Testament. He explains:

> The Gospel of John begins with an extraordinary poetic, mystical vision of the healing of humanity, which in some way condenses the history of salvation and serves as a capsule version of the whole of this gospel. It is called the "Prologue." It is centered on the Greek word "Logos," which is normally translated as the "Word." This is not incorrect, but "Logos" has a much wider meaning, referring not only to the spoken word but also to the *idea* and *thought* behind the spoken word, the *vision*, the *plan*, and the *wisdom that inspired it. It is the "Word" that has the power to change, create and transform. "Wisdom" and "Word" both describe divine activity.*[34]

Vanier then connects the Wisdom passages from Proverbs 8 with a paraphrase of John 1: "*Before all things were, the Word was and the Word (or Wisdom) was with God (or turned towards God, present to God, in communion with God). He was God. Before all things were made he was in communion with God. All things were made through him and without him nothing was made that was made.*"[35]

In the prologue to the gospel of John, the author makes several poetic parallels between Wisdom and Jesus the Living Word, which resonate with

---

31. Ibid., 47.

32. Origen, *Origen, On First Principles,* 110.

33. Augustine, *On the Trinity,* 164.

34. Vanier, *Drawn into the Mystery of Jesus through the Gospel of John,* 18. (Italics in the original.)

35. Ibid., 18. (Italics in the original.)

other New Testament writers. For example, Proverbs identifies Wisdom as the path that ensures life (4:11, 22, 26), and John 14:6 identifies Jesus Christ as the Way of life. Likewise, the references to Jesus as the Wisdom of God (Luke 11:49, 1 Cor 1:24; Matt 11:19) echo the claims made in Proverbs 8:23–31 about Wisdom.

Elizabeth Johnson summarizes the connections between Jesus and Wisdom as follows:

> What Judaism said of Sophia, Christian hymn makers and epistle writers now came to say of Jesus: he is the image of the invisible God (Col 1:15); the radiant light of God's glory (Heb 1:3); the firstborn of all creation (Col 1:15); the one through whom all things were made (1 Cor 8:6). Likewise, the way in which Judaism characterized Sophia in her dealings with human beings, Gospel writers now come to portray Jesus: he calls out to heavy burdened to come to him and find rest (Matt 11:28–30); he makes people friends of God (John 15:15), and gifts those who love him with life (John 17:2).[36]

The theological connection between Lady Wisdom and the Logos is also reflected in ancient art and architecture. As Edwina Gately and Robert Lantz observe in *Christ in the Margins*, "In the Byzantine Church, these references to Wisdom are considered references to Christ. Churches like Hagia Sophia [Holy Wisdom] in Istanbul are dedicated to Christ."[37] These authors go on to explain that in many icons Jesus is painted as an "androgynous figure, with Mary on one side and John the Baptist on the other. Thus before the incarnation the second person of the Trinity was seen as 'she' but for cultural reasons became a man."[38]

Thus in earlier times Wisdom and Christ were seen much more interchangeably. Today, in Eastern Orthodoxy, the Hagia Sophia churches symbolize "the ideas of Wisdom as God's feminine Presence and the church as the maternal womb of reborn Christians. The modern Russian Orthodox theologian Sergius Bugakov has developed the Eastern theology of Wisdom. . . . Wisdom is the ground of being of the three persons of God."[39]

---

36. Johnson, *She Who Is*, 95. Johnson also references other writers who have come to a similar conclusion: James Dunn identifies Jesus as "the exhaustive embodiment of divine wisdom"; M. Jack Suggs argues that the gospel of Matthew portrays Jesus as "Sophia incarnate"; Raymond Brown argues that the gospel of John personifies Jesus as Wisdom.

37. Gately and Lantz, *Christ in the Margins*, 113.

38. Ibid.

39. Ruether, *Mary*, 38.

Similarly, the Catholic understanding of Wisdom is informed by The Book of Wisdom, which is missing from protestant Bibles but found in the Apocrypha. Here Wisdom is described in detail:

> For within her is a spirit intelligent, holy, unique, manifold, subtle, mobile, incisive, unsullied, lucid, invulnerable, benevolent, shrewd, irresistible, beneficent, friendly to human beings, steadfast, dependable, unperturbed, almighty, all-surveying, penetrating all intelligent, pure and most subtle spirits. For Wisdom is quicker to move than any motion; she is so pure, she pervades and permeates all things. She is a breath of the power of God, pure emanation of the glory of the Almighty; so nothing impure can find its way into her. For she is a reflection of the eternal light, untarnished mirror of God's active power, and image of his goodness. Although she is alone, she can do everything; herself unchanging, she renews the world, and, generation after generation, passing into holy souls, she makes them into God's friends and prophets. (Wisdom 7:22–27, *New Jerusalem Bible*)

Jewish tradition has a more elevated understanding of Lady Wisdom as well, with Song of Songs being described as a love song between Solomon and Lady Wisdom, and some suggesting that Lady Wisdom is wooing her lover.[40]

THE WOMB OF THE FATHER

"In the beginning, God birthed the heavens and the earth." So John Goldingay interprets the first verse of the Bible. He refers to Psalm 90:2, "before mountains were birthed, or you labored with earth and world,"[41] and explains "Birthing is an image that tells us something true about God's relationship to the world."[42] First, he says, "birthing suggests wondrous mystery." Second, birthing involves pain and struggle. "It hints at risk, because birthing is not bound to succeed and may bring death to the mother. But it also hints at joy."[43] He explains further that the word translated "labored with" can mean "dancing or whirling but most often refers to the twisting

---

40. See, for example, Goldingay, "Song of Songs."

41. Goldingay, *Old Testament Theology*, 61.

42. Ibid., 61.

43. Ibid., 62.

and straining involved in giving birth."[44] Thus Goldingay is implying that what Hebrews would hear in Genesis 1 and Psalm 90 would be resonance with God giving birth.

There is also a marked fluidity between female and male images for God in the gospel of St. John, which we see reflected in John's opening line: "In the beginning was the Word, and the Word was with God, and the Word was God." This resonance of Word and wisdom, as noted above, also echoes the beginning of Genesis, where *ruach* hovers over the earth. This association of the feminine Spirit and rebirth is especially explicit in John 3:4, where Nicodemus asks Jesus, "'How can a man be born when he is old? He cannot enter a second time into his mother's womb and be born, can he?'" In verses 5–8, Jesus responds to Nicodemus's question about re-entering the womb by saying, "'Truly, truly, I say to you, unless one is born of water and the Spirit he cannot enter into the kingdom of God. That which is born of the flesh is flesh, and that which is born of the Spirit is spirit. Do not be amazed that I said to you, 'You must be born again.' The wind blows where it wishes and you hear the sound of it, but do not know where it comes from and where it is going; so is everyone who is born of the Spirit.'"

This reference to entering the womb and being born of the Spirit echoes back to the opening chapter of the gospel, where, in the earliest Syriac version, John refers to "the only-begotten Son, which is from the womb of the Father" (1:18).[45] Yet this connection to the womb of the father is often lost in translation, for in the New American Version, this same passage reads: "the only begotten God who is in the bosom of the Father." Yet John clearly had such a connection in mind, since the Greek word *kolpon*, which is translated here as "bosom," is the same word he used in the dialogue between Nicodemus and Jesus in John 3:3–4, when Jesus tells Nicodemus he must be born again and Nicodemus asks "He cannot enter a second time into his mother's womb and be born, can he?"

Later in the fourth century, Ephren drew on this image of God's womb, "whence the Son departed for the womb of Mary."[46] He connects the image of the Son who leaves the Father's womb for the womb of Mary and then gives birth to all of humanity through the waters of baptism. (Baptism is connected to the waters of birth, and baptismal fonts were often womb-shaped.) This concept of the womb of the Father is echoed in Vanier's

44. Ibid, 62.

45. Harvey, "Female Imagery for the Divine," 126.

46. Ibid., 133.

paraphrase of John 1:18: "*No one has ever seen God except the only begotten Son who was in the womb of the Father. He has made God known.* Or as Luc de Villers, a professor at L'Ecole Biblique de Jerusalem translates it, *The only Son of God who came to lead us into the womb of the Father.*"[47]

NAMING GOD: EL SHADDAI

There are numerous names for God throughout the Old Testament that signify attributes of God's character, such as: Provider, Most High, Protector, Redeemer, the Lord God of Heaven. The most common names were *El* (God) and *Jahweh*, the most sacred name, which was never pronounced in everyday life. This name, which is derived from *hayah* (to be), refers to the "I am who I am" of Exodus 3:14–15 and 6:3.[48] This name was so holy that it was only spoken by the high priest on the Day of Atonement. Because this name was so sacred, it was represented in the Scriptures by only four consonants (JHWH), or else replaced with LORD or Adonai. It is also said to represent the breath—in and out for each syllable—which connects Jahweh with *Ruach* (Spirit).

Many of the names of God have masculine connotations, and many others are without gender. El Shaddai, a name that could well be feminine, has created some controversy. Though usually translated as Almighty (Shaddai) God (El), Scofield's commentary offers another perspective: "The etymological signification of Almighty God (El Shaddai) is both interesting and touching. God (El) signifies the 'Strong One.' The qualifying word Shaddai is formed from the Hebrew word 'shad,' the breast, invariably used in Scripture for a woman's breast. Shaddai therefore means primarily 'the breasted.' God is 'Shaddai,' because He is the Nourisher, the Strength-giver."[49] Similarly, as *The Inclusive Bible* explains in a footnote, "There is growing opinion, however, that Shaddai may derive from the word shad or 'breast'—thus El Shaddai may be a feminine image of God meaning 'the Breasted God.'"[50] Thus El Shaddai has a strong feminine connotation, but it

47. Vanier, *Drawn into the Mystery,* 21. (Italics in the original.)

48. Exod 6:3 says, in effect, "I appeared to Abraham, Isaac and Jacob as El Shaddai but to you as JHWH."

49. Scofield, *Bibletools,* Lines 5–9, 11–13.

50. "The name El Shaddai is usually translated 'the Almighty,' under the assumption that it derives either from the word *shadad*, which means 'burly' or 'powerful,' or from *shadah*, which means 'mountain,' making the name mean 'God of the mountains.' There

is not translated as such in most Bibles. Yet *The Inclusive Bible*, because of its commitment to gender accuracy, translates the six references to El Shaddai in Genesis as "the Breasted One." For example, Genesis 49:25 reads: "through the God of your ancestors who aids you, by the Breasted One who blesses you: the blessings of Heaven on high, the blessings of the Deep down below, the blessings of breasts and womb."[51]

Contemporary hermeneutics emphasizes that the translator must not only look at the root meaning of a word for accurate translation, but also the context. The six times El Shaddai is used in Genesis are telling, as they refer to fruitfulness, increase in numbers, blessings of the breast and womb, and, in once case, mercy. Thus the translation of El Shaddai as the Breasted One has both etymological and contextual accuracy.[52]

Job uses the name El Shaddai more than any other book of Scripture (thirty-one times). The Job passages follow a poetic pattern of "God . . . the Almighty . . ." as though contrasting the two names of God, El and Shaddai. For example, Job 5:17 follows this contrasting pattern: "Look, happy is the person whom God rebukes, so don't reject Shaddai's discipline." These names do not seem to have a particularly feminine connotation, but the writer of Job might be establishing a poetic pattern, where one name is more masculine and the other is more feminine.[53]

---

is growing opinion, however, that Shaddai may derive from the word *shad* or 'breast'— thus El Shaddai may be a feminine image of God meaning 'the Breasted God.' Then again, since mountains are frequently shaped liked breasts, these two interpretations are not mutually exclusive."

51. *The Inclusive Bible.*

52. The other verses in *The Inclusive Bible* version of Genesis are: Gen 17:1–2 ("When Abram was ninety-nine years old, YHWH appeared and said, 'I am the Breasted One. Walk in my presence and be blameless. I will make a covenant between you and me, and I will increase your numbers exceedingly'"); 28:3 ("May the Breasted One bless you; may God make you fruitful and increase your descendants until they become a family of nations"); 35:11 ("God said to him, 'I am the Breasted One, Bear fruit, and increase your numbers! A nation—a host of nations!—will descend from you, and rulers will also spring from you'"); 43:14 ("May the Breasted One be merciful to you before the official, so that he will allow both the one you left behind and Benjamin to return with you. As for me, if I must grieve, I will grieve"); 48:3–4 ("Jacob said to Joseph, 'The Breasted One appeared to me at Luz in the land of Canaan, and blessed me. God told me, 'I will make you bear fruit and will increase your descendants until they become a multitude of nations, and I will give this land to your descendants to have forever'").

53. For further examples of this pattern, see the following passages from Job, which are all quoted from *The Inclusive Bible*: 8:3 ("Does God pervert justice? Does Shaddai pervert what the truth?"); 8:5 ("Now if you look to God and plead with Shaddai"); 11:17 ("Can you uncover the mystery of the divine? Can you discover the limits of Shaddai?");

El Shaddai also appears twice in Numbers,[54] twice in Ruth,[55] twice in Psalms,[56] once in Isaiah,[57] twice in Ezekiel,[58] and once in Joel.[59] As this overview of the Scriptures containing El Shaddai suggests, there is a feminine resonance in the images of God as the Breasted One, nurturer and provider. Yet some of these verses convey destruction rather than nurturing protection. Thus the Hebrew listener would have recognized the feminine connotations while remaining aware of the fluid presence of both genders in the Godhead.

SHEKINAH

The word *Shekinah*, which refers to the presence of God, is defined by the *Jewish Encyclopedia* as: "The majestic presence or manifestation of God which has descended to 'dwell' among men . . . The word itself is taken from such passages as speak of God dwelling either in the Tabernacle or among

---

13:3 ("It is to Shaddai alone that I would speak—I intend to make my case before God"); 22:26 ("Then you'll dwell in the embrace of Shaddai and lift up your face to God"); 27:13 ("This is the destiny the wicked receive from God the inheritance the ruthless receive from Shaddai"); 31:12 ("But what is our agreement with God above? What are we promised from Shaddai, from on high?"); 33:4 ("The Spirit of God is what made me; the breath of Shaddai gives me life").

54. Num 24:4 ("the prophecy of one who hears the words of God: I see what the Breasted One makes me see; God answers me, and opens my eyes.) Num 24:16 ("the prophecy of one who hears the words of God, who has knowledge of YHWH: I see what YHWH makes me see; God answers me, and opens my eyes.")

55. "But she said to them, 'Don't call me Naomi. Call me Mara, 'Bitterness,' for YHWH has afflicted me, and Shaddai has brought bitter destruction on me. I was filled to the brim when I departed, but YHWH has brought me back empty. Why insist on calling me Naomi, since YHWH has passed sentence upon me and Shaddai has brought me to ruin?'" (Ruth 1:20–21).

56. "When Shaddai scattered the rulers in Zalmon, it looked like a snowstorm had swept through" (Ps 68:14). "You who dwell in the shelter of the Most High and pass the night in the shadow of Shaddai" (Ps 91:1). This second verse has a feminine connotation, as it is followed by the image of the bird under whose wings we can take refuge.

57. "Wail, for the day of YHWH comes! Destruction is coming from El Shaddai—the Breasted God!" (Isa 13:6).

58. "When the creatures moved, their wings made a noise like the roar of rushing waters, like the voice of the Breasted God, like the din of a moving army" Ezek 1:24). "The sound of the wings of the cherubim could be heard as far away as the outer court, like the voice of the Breasted God when speaking" (Ezek 10:5).

59. "Agh, the Day! The Day of YHWH is coming! It will arrive as a great upheaval from the Breasted One" (Joel 1:15).

the people of Israel."[60] See, for example, Exodus 25:8,[61] Psalm 135:21,[62] and Ezekiel 43:7.[63] Further, "Since the Shekinah is light, those passages of the Apocrypha and New Testament which mention radiance . . . refer to the Shekinah,"[64] as in the glory of the Lord shone round about them (Luke 2:9).

While not an actual biblical word, Shekinah is a biblical concept that has a feminine connotation that Hebrew people would have understood. Holly Snead writes,

> "Shekinah, The Presence of Divinity" speaks of a maternal aspect of God that was present from the first day of creation and is still essential today. Shekinah is a Talmudic term describing the abiding presence of God on earth. Many Hebrews understand Shekinah as the 'mother' or feminine presence of God, closely connected with the Sophia Wisdom of God found in Proverbs 1:20 . . . The Gender of the subject in the Hebrew plays an important role in sentence structure. "The glorious Shekinah returned to bless us" does not reveal gender in English. In Hebrew, however, verbs and adjectives have male and female forms and suggest gender. In Hebrew, this sentence indicates three times that Shekinah is female.[65]

This chapter has traced explicit and implicit representations of the feminine Divine. The many implicit references to the feminine would be heard by Hebrew listeners, but not by English speakers. These images and word associations would reverberate with the presence of a tender and protective feminine presence. More explicitly, El Shaddai as a female name for God has been disguised in most English translations of our Bibles, and yet the association with the breast and the womb is so clear that *The Inclusive Bible* has translated the name as the Breasted One.

While masculine, or at least general parental naming is more common, the feminine is powerfully present in the original language. Nevertheless, our God remains mystery beyond our mortal minds and complexity who can be understood only dimly. May we find more deeply the richness of our God who, like "the dove that flies," spreads her wings over us all.

---

60. Kohler and Blau, "Shekinah," line 1.

61. "Let them construct a sanctuary for Me, that I may dwell among them."

62. "Blessed be the Lord from Zion, who dwells in Jerusalem."

63. "He said to me, 'Son of man, this is the place of My throne and the place of the soles of My feet, where I will dwell among the sons of Israel forever.'"

64. Kohler and Blau, "Shekinah: In the Apocrypha and New Testament," line 1.

65. Snead, *The Holy Days of God, the Holidays of Man*, 175.

The early seventeenth-century poet and preacher John Donne expresses something of this wonder:

> My God, my God, thou art a direct God . . . But thou art a figurative, a metaphoric God too: a God in whose words there is such a height of figures, such voyages, such peregrinations to fetch remote and precious metaphors, such extensions, such spreadings, such curtains of allegories, such third heavens of hyperboles, so harmonious elocutions, so refined and so reserved expressions, so commanding persuasions, so persuading commandments . . . thou art the dove that flies.[66]

---

66. Donne, *Devotions upon Emergent Occasions*, 124.

3

Church Fathers, Mystics, and *She Who Is*

Jesus, as a mother you gather your people to you,
you are gentle with us as a mother with her children.
Often you weep over our sins and our pride,
tenderly you draw us from hatred and judgement.
You comfort us in sorrow and bind up our wounds,
in sickness you nurse us and with pure milk you feed us.[1]

In this chapter, I explore the language and conceptualizations of the feminine Divine in church tradition. In the early centuries of the church's life, it was common for the church fathers to use feminine metaphors when speaking of God. In fact, in Syriac Christianity, the Holy Spirit was referred to in feminine terms for the first few centuries of the early church. These terms and metaphors for the Trinity continued to be used by both men and women through the centuries. Mystics employed ecstatic language to express their longings and union with God, which necessarily relied on gendered terms. In the twelfth and thirteenth centuries, knights and troubadours often sang romantic and even erotic courtly love songs to a noble lady—not a lover, but rather an inspiration for whom they were willing to

---

1. Anselm, *The Prayers and Meditations of Saint Anselm*, 155.

go to battle. This idealizing of a lady was reflected in the language of female representations of God, such as Lady Poverty.

THE TRINITY AS MOTHER

Speaking of God in motherly language was common in the early Christian centuries amongst the church fathers, who often referred to suckling at the breast of God or drinking of the milk of Christ. Clement of Alexandria (AD 150–215) writes of God as being mother and woman for us: "For what is more essential to God than the mystery of love? Look then into the womb (*kolpon*) of the Father, Which alone has brought forth the only-begotten Son of God . . . God is love, and for love of us has become woman (*ethēlynthē*). The ineffable being of the Father has out of compassion with us become mother. By loving, the Father has become woman (*Agapēsas ho Patēr ethēlynthē*)."[2]

Further, from Syriac Christianity, we have the following: "The world considers you a merciful mother. Bring with you calm and peace, and spread your wings over our sinful times."[3] Until about AD 400, Syriac, Hebrew and Aramaic (the language Jesus spoke) almost always used the feminine form when speaking of the Holy Spirit. This is the norm in the three major writings of early Syriac literature: the Acts of Thomas and the writings of Aphrahat, and Ephrem. Ephrem uses female imagery for each person of the Trinity—the Father as Divinity's womb, Christ as the mother, and the feminine form for the Holy Spirit.[4] In his *Hymns on the Nativity*, Ephrem draws out the feminine metaphors: "the Father and the Son weave garments as a woman does; God the Father works as a housekeeper. There are many references to God's wings vividly reminiscent of the bird imagery noted above for the Spirit."[5] Another example of the fluidity of feminine imagery is demonstrated in the following hymn by Ephrem: "He is the Living Breast of living breath; by His life the dead were suckled, and they revived . . . As indeed he sucked Mary's milk, He has given suck—life to the

---

2. Clement of Alexandria, *Patrologia Graeca*, col. 641, cited in Swidler, *Biblical Affirmations of Woman*, 66.

3. Johnson, *Women, Earth and Creator Spirit*, 56.

4. Ephrem, *Ephrem the Syrian: Hymns*, 10.

5. Harvey, "Female Imagery for the Divine," 133.

universe. As again he dwelt in His mother's womb, in His womb dwells all creation."[6]

Virginia Mollenkott notes the following church fathers who use the biblical images of God as female:

> Like Clement, St. John Chrysostom (347–407 A.D.) uses allusions to God's motherhood in his *Homilies on the Gospel of Saint Matthew*. In his *Baptismal Instructions* Chrysostom says that "Just as a woman nurtures her offspring with her own blood and milk, so also Christ continuously nurtures with His own blood and milk those whom He has begotten." At about the same time in the West, Saint Ambrose of Milan speaks of "the Father's womb" and even of the nourishing breasts of Christ. And in the early fifth century, the Bishop of Ptolemais in Libya, Synesius, said of the Christian divinity, "You are Father, You are Mother, You are male, and You are female." Others in the orthodox Christian tradition who utilize one or several biblical images of God as female include Valentius (2nd century), Saint Gregory of Nyssa (d. about 395), Saint Augustine of Hippo (d. 430), the Venerable Bede (c. 673–735), Peter Lombard (1110–1164), Thomas Aquinas (1225–1274), St Bonaventure (1221–1274), and St. Gregory Palama (d. 1359).[7]

She comments, "By utilizing imagery of God as female, they were very simply following the usage of Scripture and the guidance of their own inner experience."[8]

However, over the centuries, the use of mother imagery dwindled. As Johnson explains, "In time most of this maternal imagery migrated away from the Spirit and accrued to the church, called Holy Mother the Church, or to Mary the mother of Jesus, venerated as mother of the faithful as well."[9] In the next chapter, I will discuss the church's shift to focus on Mary as a representation of the Divine. Yet in the twelfth and thirteenth centuries, there was a specific devotion to Jesus as mother, which was inspired perhaps by the writing of Anselm of Canterbury (1033–1109). Writing on prayer, he writes, "'run under the wings of Jesus your Mother and lament your grief under his feathers. Ask that your wounds may be healed and that, comforted, you may live again.'" As Charles Ringma notes, "This prayer recognizes the importance of shelter, nurture and homecoming in

---

6. Ephrem, *Ephrem the Syrian: Hymns,* 100.

7. Mollenkott, *The Divine Feminine,* 9.

8. Ibid., 10.

9. Johnson, *Women, Earth and Creator Spirit,* 56.

the healing process. The language in this prayer is significantly feminine, relational and profoundly healing."[10]

Such feminine images are particularly common among the Cistercian monks, including Bernard of Clairvaux (d. 1153); Aelred of Rievaulx (d. 1167); Guerric of Igny (d. about 1157); Isaac of Stella (d. about 1169); Adam of Perseigne (d. about 1221); and William of St. Thierry (d. about 1148). In writing about these monks, Bynum notes, "Each uses maternal imagery to express an intense emotional dependence of the child-soul on God."[11] She continues by describing some specific aspects of this motherly imagery: "God as a woman nursing the soul at her breasts, drying its tears, punishing its petty mischief-making, giving birth to it in agony and travail, are part of a growing tendency to speak of the divine in homey images and to emphasize its approachability."[12] Bynum summarizes three particular stereotypes: "The female is generative (the foetus is made of her very matter) and sacrificial in her generation (birth pangs); the female is loving and tender (a mother cannot help loving her own child); the female is nurturing (she feeds the child with her own bodily fluid)."[13] These medieval writers recognize the depth and fundamentally instinctive nature of maternal love, where the mother offers life to her child and gives of her very substance in birth and nurture. They draw parallels with God, who dies in self-sacrifice in order to draw her children into life. Bynum reflects on how these maternal names for God invite people to approach God as one who is accessible, human, and even "homey." Thus the use of female images for God as both Creator and Incarnation draw us into deeper intimacy with the Divine.

These ancient writers not only consider God as mother, but they also refer to Jesus as mother. Anselm, Archbishop of Canterbury, prays the following to Jesus:

> Jesus, as a mother you gather your people to you,
> you are gentle with us as a mother with her children.
> Often you weep over our sins and our pride,
> tenderly you draw us from hatred and judgement.
> You comfort us in sorrow and bind up our wounds,
> in sickness you nurse us and with pure milk you feed us.
> Jesus, by your dying, we are born to new life,

10. Ringma, *Hear the Ancient Wisdom*, 63.
11. Bynum, *Jesus as Mother*, 164.
12. Ibid., 129.
13. Ibid., 131.

by your anguish and labour we come forth in joy.
Despair turns to hope through your sweet goodness,
through your gentleness, we find comfort in fear. . .
Lord Jesus, in your mercy heal us,
in your love and tenderness, remake us.
In your compassion, bring grace and forgiveness,
for the beauty of heaven, may your love prepare us.[14]

Later writers drew on these earlier texts as well as the Scriptures to elucidate similar ideas. In speaking of the Trinity, Julian of Norwich (1342–1416) writes: "For the almighty truth of the Trinity is our Father: for he made us and keeps us in him. And the deep wisdom of the Trinity is our Mother, in whom we are enclosed. And the high goodness of the Trinity is our Lord, and in him we are enclosed and he in us . . . almighty, all wisdom, all goodness, one God, one Lord."[15]

Later theologians then drew on the church fathers. For example, John Donne (1572–1631), the Anglican priest and poet, draws from Saint John Chrysostom when he writes, "God was their father . . . and *their mother* too. . . It was a mother's part to give them suck, and to feed them with temporal blessings; it was a father's part to instruct them with spiritual things; and God did both abundantly. Therefore doth God submit himself to the comparison of a mother in the prophet Esay [Isaiah], *Can a woman forget her sucking child?*"[16] Thus throughout the centuries, we find examples of God as mother and the naming of the feminine Divine for the fullness of the Trinity.

THE HOLY SPIRIT AS MOTHER

Even though the naming of the Holy Spirit as feminine dwindled after the first centuries, Count Nikolaus Ludwig von Zinzendorf (1700–1760) and his followers, the Moravians, "prayed to the Trinity as Father, Mother, and Husband in addition to the orthodox Father, Son, and Holy Spirit."[17]

For more than thirty years, the Moravians in Europe and America used litanies that used overt feminine language. "Zinzendorf acknowledged that this type of language for the Holy Spirit was not common, but he always

14. Anselm, *The Prayers and Meditations of Saint Anselm,* 155.

15. Julian of Norwich, *Showings,* 285.

16. Donne, *The Works of John Donne,* 162–163.

17. Atwood, "The Union of Masculine and Feminine in Zinzendorfian Piety," 12.

insisted that this was the simplest, clearest, and best way to communicate the nature of the Holy Spirit. Traditional theology taught that the Holy Spirit was the comforter and giver of life, which are maternal roles. If the Spirit plays the role of a mother in the church, the Spirit should be called Mother."[18] He claimed that he had little conscious awareness of the Holy Spirit until midlife, when he learned to call on the Spirit as Mother. For him the traditional church language used for the Holy Spirit was "abstract to the point of meaninglessness,"[19] whereas naming her as Mother identified the real way she related to God's children. He was not rejecting the Christian understanding of the Trinity, but clarifying the specific motherly roles that the Holy Spirit played. He stated, "God [Christ] is even our dear husband, his Father is our dear father, and the Holy Spirit is our dear Mother."[20]

The naming of the Holy Spirit as Mother facilitated a more intimate way of relating with God, and it helped men to see themselves in a less stereotypically "masculine" way. In this way, Moravian men were able to model themselves on a:

> tradition of "vulnerable masculinity" that had had long been available as a gender role within spiritual communities . . . A model of vulnerable masculinity can, of course, be found in the image of the wounded Christ of the Passion. For the Moravians, this is a Christ who retains a dominant appearance of masculinity, but with what one could call feminine marks . . . this Moravian Jesus is not female but eternally male, eternally vulnerable and male, and signifies not just a cultural struggle between "radical pietism" and orthodox Lutheranism, but an important moment of crisis and transition in the history of masculinity.[21]

Thus the Moravians were not only naming the Holy Spirit as mother, but also recognizing the intertwined effect of this naming on their understanding of masculinity, their gender roles, and their sexuality.

Such examples point toward the ease with which many in the long tradition of the church related to God as Mother. Clearly, in past centuries, maternal images of God were part of mainstream orthodoxy. Moreover, throughout these centuries, mystics expressed their intimate relationships to God with ecstasy, often turning to sexual language.

18. Ibid., 12–13.

19. Ibid., 13.

20. Ibid., 14.

21. Faull, "Temporal Men and the Eternal Bridegroom," 56.

UNION WITH GOD AS EROTIC

Throughout Christendom, men and women have longed for intimacy with God and have recognized that this yearning has its source in God. Because the mystery of union with God, the creator of the cosmos, defies ordinary language, writers often turn to erotic images and terms. In "The Body's Grace," Rowan Williams, the previous Archbishop of Canterbury, follows many of the mystics by recognizing that our desire for God originates in God's prior desire for us. "The whole story of creation, incarnation, and our incorporation into the fellowship of Christ's body tells us that God desires us, *as if we were God,* as if we were that unconditional response to God's giving that God's self makes in the life of the Trinity. We are created so that we may be caught up in this, so that we may grow into the wholehearted love of God by learning that God loves us as God loves God."[22]

For women, the possibility of a romantic/erotic relationship with God has been more straightforward, as they have been able to identify with the erotic language of the lover and beloved in the Song of Solomon. Men have approached this lover-beloved relationship in a variety of ways, either by identifying themselves as feminine in response to a male lover, or by using motherly language that subtly refers to God's breasts and womb, or by representing God as a feminine lover.

Some of the erotic and sensual language is implied rather than explicit. For example, Origen (184–254) views *eros* as "a crucial part of expressing the human soul's deep, yearning desire for God. Origen suggests that *eros* love is so passionate and so deep that we are somehow 'wounded' by it. Referring to Christ as a 'dart', and picturing Christ's love for humanity as erotic, Origen suggests that Christ himself 'pierces' and 'wounds' those who experience this love."[23] Reflecting on Song of Songs 2:5 ("for I am wounded by love," or "sick with love"), Origen explains: "If there is anyone who has been pierced with the loveworthy spear of [Christ's] knowledge, so that he yearns and longs for him by day and night, can speak of naught but him, would hear of naught but him, can think of nothing else, and is disposed to no desire nor longing nor yet hope, except for him alone—if such there be, that soul then says in truth: 'I have been wounded by love.'"[24]

22. Williams, "The Body's Grace," 311–12.

23. Cornwall, *Theology and Sexuality,* 34–35.

24. Origen, *The Song of Songs,* 198.

Augustine of Hippo, who is sometimes considered a misogynist who belittled women, also uses sensual language for God. In his Confessions, he writes,

> Late have I loved Thee, O beauty so ancient and so new; late have I loved Thee! For behold Thou wert within me, and I outside; and I sought Thee outside and in my unloveliness fell upon those lovely things that Thou hast made. Thou wert with me and I was not with Thee. I was kept from Thee by those things, yet had they not been in Thee, they would not have been at all. Thou didst call and cry to me and break open my deafness: and Thou didst send forth Thy beams and shine upon me and chase away my blindness: Thou didst breathe fragrance upon me, and I drew in breath and do now pant for Thee: I tasted Thee: and now hunger and thirst for Thee: Thou didst touch me, and I have burned for Thy peace.[25]

Thus Augustine, who calls Christ mother, also employs sensuous and erotic language in his prayers to God.

Male as Feminine Beloved

The rapturous language that Augustine employs in the above passage is free from gender references. Because such erotic language is almost always gendered, men often find it difficult to engage with these images. Yet through the centuries, some men have solved this by identifying with the feminine. "If the God with whom [religious males] wished to unite was spoken of in male language, it was hard to use the metaphor of sexual union unless they saw themselves as female . . . We also have many examples of monks describing themselves or their souls as the brides of Christ, that is, female."[26] One well-known example is St. John of the Cross (1542–1591), whose beautiful poem, "The Dark Night," demonstrates the erotic union of lover and beloved:

> One dark night,
> fired with love's urgent longings
> —ah, the sheer grace!—
> I went out unseen,
> my house being now all stilled.

---

25. Augustine, *The Confessions of Saint Augustine*, 188–89.
26. Bynum, *Jesus as Mother*, 161.

In darkness, and secure,
by the secret ladder, disguised,
—ah, the sheer grace!—
in darkness and concealment,
my house being now all stilled.

On that glad night,
in secret, for no one saw me,
nor did I look at anything,
with no other light or guide
than the one that burned in my heart.

This guided me
more surely than the light of noon
to where he was awaiting me
—him I knew so well—
there in a place where no one appeared.

O guiding night!
O night more lovely than the dawn!
O night that has united
the Lover with his beloved,
transforming the beloved in her Lover.

Upon my flowering breast
which I kept wholly for him alone,
there he lay sleeping,
and I caressing him
there in a breeze from the fanning cedars.

When the breeze blew from the turret,
as I parted his hair,
it wounded my neck
with its gentle hand,
suspending all my senses.

I abandoned and forgot myself,
laying my face on my Beloved;
all things ceased; I went out from myself,
leaving my cares
forgotten among the lilies.[27]

27. Kavanagh and Rodriguez, *Collected Works of St. John of the Cross*, 358.

In this poem, St. John identifies himself with the feminine beloved in order to employ erotic language to express the depth of his intimacy and ecstasy with the Divine.

Maternal Erotic Imagery

Other male writers allude to the erotic more subtly by using maternal imagery that focuses on the breasts and the womb. As Caroline Bynum observes,

> But another solution (which kept images drawn from human relationships central and did not require the male to describe himself in a female image) was of course to see God as female parent with whom union could be quite physical (in the womb or at the breast.) We should not ignore the possibility that in such writings males could express as males certain sexual desires: play at the breast and entry into the female body . . . Throughout the Middle Ages, authors . . . were clearly not embarrassed to speak of all kinds of ecstasy in language we find physical and sexual and therefore inappropriate for God.[28]

Yet many people fear that using feminine or erotic language for the Divine might spark "dangerous" sexual energy that could result in inappropriate behavior or imagining. Some of Zinzendorf's followers experienced this when the invitation to call the Holy Spirit "mother" led to erotic/romantic imagery and freedom in human sexual relationships. As Craig Atwood observes, "Zinzendorf described religious experience in terms similar to falling in love. 'And as soon as they are with him, there is an embrace, a kiss, a heart, thus he draws like a magnet, rises them all up to himself, lays them deep in his holy side, so that a soul in that hour and at that moment when she has experienced it can say: much happiness to eternal life, if only my whole life could remain like this!'"[29] This acceptance of the goodness of sexuality and gender affected their own romantic relationships. "They proclaimed that the bodies of men and women were blessed by God and that the incarnation of Christ had removed all shame associated with the body. Salvation was described in erotic terms of union with God, and sexual intercourse in marriage was celebrated as a form of liturgy."[30]

28. Bynum, *Jesus as Mother,* 161–62.

29. Atwood, "The Union of Masculine and Feminine," 20.

30. Ibid., 12.

It is possible that this freedom progressed further for unmarried young people also, although little is recorded of these outcomes.

Symbolic Feminine Lover: Lady Poverty, Lady Compassion

Some men have engaged the feminine Divine romantically through a symbolic marriage partner, such as Lady Poverty, Lady Compassion, or Mary, the mother of Jesus. In the next chapter, I will explore Mary as a representation of the Divine. In the remaining section of this chapter, I will focus on Lady Poverty and Lady Compassion as feminine representations of God.

Francis of Assisi (1182–1226) spoke of Lady Poverty as a Divine lover. Before abandoning his life of revelry and privilege, his companions asked him if he would be married. "Yes," he replied, "I am about to take a wife of surpassing fairness."[31] His marriage was to poverty as a way of life. Bonaventure, Francis's biographer, describes the profound romantic relationship that Francis had with Lady Poverty: "He saw that poverty was the close companion of the Son of God, and now that it was rejected by the whole world, he was eager to espouse it in everlasting love. For the sake of poverty he not only left his father and his mother, but also gave away everything he had."[32] In the following, Bonaventure describes a vision Francis had:

> he was met by three poor women who were exactly alike in height, age and appearance. They offered him the gift of a new salutation, saying: "Welcome, Lady Poverty!" When he heard this, the true lover of poverty was filled with unspeakable joy because there was nothing in him that he would rather have people acknowledge than what these women singled out . . . It seemed that these three poor women who were so alike in appearance, who gave such an unusual greeting and disappeared suddenly, appropriately showed that the beauty of Gospel perfection, in poverty, chastity, and obedience shone forth perfectly equal in the man of God although he had chosen to glory above all in the privilege of poverty which he used to call his mother, his bride, and his lady.[33]

In this vision, the three women echo the Trinity, who identify and welcome within Francis his beloved bride, Lady Poverty. Juniper, one of the Franciscan brothers, describes his own tumultuous relationship with Lady

31. Matheson, *Icons of the Middle* Ages, 329.

32. Bonaventure, *The Life of Saint Francis*, 239.

33. Ibid., 243–44.

Poverty. On the one hand, he hates the feeling of dependence on others resulting from his vow of poverty, but on the other, this dependence brings freedom: "If I am truly poor, then I am dependent on others for everything, and I feel useless and worthless, and I realize deep within that everything is a gift from the Father. Then in this attitude of complete dependence, I become useful again, for then I am empty of selfishness and I am free to be God's instrument instead of my own."[34]

Nevertheless he finds this dependence painful: "I write these words in pain, Lady Poverty, for I have wept bitter tears because I was poor and had to beg from others, and I felt like a burden to people and to God."[35] Like Francis, Juniper addresses Lady Poverty as his beloved:

> Lady Poverty, I love you. You, my Lady, take all the sting from being poor. In your embrace I am rich indeed, for I have someone to love. I have you. Perhaps, my Lady, that is why I keep submitting, surrendering my desire to control my life, my need to provide for the future. You have stolen my heart and made me happy, and your love makes up for all the pain that loving you involves . . . Then we feel your embrace and we experience perfect joy; and we know it is all worthwhile because when we look into your eyes, we see Christ Himself.[36]

In the same way, Thomas Merton describes his romantic relationship with Lady Compassion: "I die of love for you, Compassion: I take you for my Lady, as Francis married poverty I marry you, the Queen of hermits and the Mother of the poor."[37] He calls himself the bridegroom of Lady Compassion and writes poetically of the love he experiences: "Love sails me around the house. I walk two steps on the ground and four steps in the air. It is love. It is consolation . . . I love God. Love carries me all around . . . I tell you, love is the only thing that makes it possible for me to continue to tick."[38]

The possibility that men (and women) could experience an intimate relationship with the Divine feminine by symbolizing God as a Lady appears historically in a number of places. It has also been suggested that the lover-beloved relationship depicted in the Song of Songs portrays the

34. Bodo, *Juniper*, 61.

35. Ibid., 61.

36. Ibid., 62–63.

37. Merton, *The Sign of Jonas*, 334.

38. Ibid., 120.

feminine beloved as Lady Wisdom. Hildegard of Bingen (1098–1179) describes Song of Songs as the love song written by Solomon when he received Divine (female) wisdom. She suggests that "he spoke . . ." to God (Lady Wisdom) "as to a woman in the familiar language of love."[39] In *The Erotic Word*, David Carr states that "some Jewish mystical works likewise used the Song of Songs to image the believer's passionate attachment to various feminine principles: the divine Torah, the in-dwelling Shekinah, and so on. In these and other ways, the Song has been a way of imagining a love relationship with a feminine divinity, and not just a way of being a woman in love with a male god."[40]

CONCLUSION

As we have seen, the church in the first centuries often identified the Holy Spirit, God, and the Trinity as feminine. Though this naming of the feminine Divine became more infrequent later in the history and life of the church, it continued to appear in the writings of godly men and women. This was particularly revealed in the writings of the church fathers, monks, and mystics, who recognized God as both mother and lover. In identifying God as lover, many of the male writers either took on a feminine identity, or they attributed to God a symbolic feminine identity. In the next chapter, we will see how the feminine Divine, which these writers attributed to the Holy Spirit and sometimes the Trinity, shifted over time to the church and then to Mary, who became a representation of divinity rather than a human mother of the Son of God.

39. Newman, *Sister of Wisdom*, 65.
40. Carr, *The Erotic Word*, 143.

4

The Crowning of Mary, Queen of Heaven

Now may every pulse of good
Seek to serve before thy face,
Virgin, Queen of Motherhood,
Keep us, Goddess, in thy grace.[1]

In this chapter, I will explore how Mary, the mother of Jesus, came to be elevated to divine status alongside the Trinity as the Queen of heaven. This shift happened over time as the church lost its feminine language for God. My purpose here is not to argue whether or not Mary is divine, but rather to recognize how thinking about Mary and the practice of praying to Mary reveals humanity's need to find the Divine feminine. For when the feminine disappeared from the church's understanding of the Trinity, Mary became elevated as an object of divine adoration in order to fulfill that human longing. I will turn to the writings of Thomas Merton, which reflect a Catholic understanding of Mary, in order to demonstrate this human need for a relationship with the feminine Divine.

---

1. Goethe, *Faust*, 266.

MARY AND THE EARLY CHURCH: CO-REDEMPTRIX

In chapter 2, I traced the frequent allusions to feminine symbols in the Old Testament and Judaism: Lady Wisdom as a symbol for God's wisdom, Israel as God's bride, Jerusalem, and Israel as a mother. "The early Christian church inherited these feminine symbols and continued to use them. At first they were adapted and developed in the new Israel quite independent of teaching about Mary as an individual. Later as Mariology developed, they were drawn in and absorbed by it."[2] In chapter 2, I also explored how in the early centuries after Christ, the Spirit was identified as feminine, and many Christians prayed to "Jesus our mother," but over time the Trinity became solely masculine. "In time most of the maternal imagery migrated away from the Spirit and accrued to the church, called Holy Mother the Church, or to Mary the mother of Jesus, venerated as mother of the faithful as well."[3]

While this shift may have allowed believers to nurture an intimate relationship with a feminine figure, it stripped the feminine away from the Divine, establishing God as more singularly masculine. As a result of this shift, Mary became a more divine figure rather than being honored as the human mother of Jesus. Mary "appears from the time of the Gospels as an integral part of the Christian mystery and as part of God's plans for the salvation of the human race. But within a few hundred years, her role in the divine mystery was substantially embellished."[4] After this time, more mythological attributes began to appear: her miraculous conception, her perpetual virginity, and her bodily assumption into heaven.

More important theologically, Mary came to be seen as the co-redeemer with Christ: the co-redemptrix.[5] Justin Martyr, an early church father, refers to Paul's writing about Adam as the one through whom many were made sinners and to Jesus as the second Adam who brought redemption (Rom 5:18–19). He adds that while Eve "conceived the word of the

---

2. Ruether, *Mary*, 36.

3. Johnson, *Women, Earth, and Creator Spirit*, 56. "The symbol of the maternity of the Spirit was virtually forgotten, along with the capacity of images of Wisdom and Shekinah to evoke divine presence and activity in female form."

4. Engelsman, *Feminine Dimension of the Divine*, 122.

5. Ibid. "The other two Mariological motifs dramatize the importance of her relationship to her son. The first was expressed in the title *Theotokos*, or Mother of God, conferred on Mary at the Council of Ephesus in 431 C.E. The second emerged from the portrait of Mary as co-redemptrix in the theology of some of the patristic fathers."

serpent, and brought forth disobedience,"[6] Mary gave birth to Jesus the Redeemer. Irenaeus (AD 130–202) is even more clear about this double typology of salvation. He writes, "And thus it also was that the knot of Eve's disobedience was loosed by the obedience of Mary. For what the Virgin Eve had bound fast through unbelief, this did the Virgin Mary set free through faith."[7] And again: "And thus, as the human race fell into bondage to death by means of a virgin, so is it rescued by a virgin, virginal disobedience having been balanced in the opposite scale by virginal obedience. For in the same way the sin of the first created man receives amendment by the correction of the First-begotten."[8] Irenaeus is clearly stating that humanity is saved by both Mary and Jesus. As Joan Englesman observes, Irenaeus is proposing "Mary as the co-redemptrix with Christ."[9]

These very early church fathers named Mary as redeemer alongside Christ. More recently, ethnic groups around the world have also honored Mary as their redeemer. The most famous example is Our Lady of Guadalupe, whom Mexican laborers continue to follow as the "Queen of Mexico" after a peasant saw an apparition of her in the fields near Mexico City in 1531. As Rosemary Radford Ruether explains, the people are drawn to the mothering divine, Mary, rather than the God of their oppressors. "The dark-skinned Virgin of Guadalupe rallies the farm workers as both a symbol of agriculture and of the oppressed dark-skinned workers of the fields. She, rather than the Christ of the Spanish conquerors, is the redeemer of the Indian people."[10] Other similar stories come from the Philippines, in which believers have seen apparitions of "Mary, Mediatrix of all Graces."[11] The Catholic Catechism states: "Taken up to heaven she did not lay aside this saving office but her manifold intercession continues to bring us the gifts of eternal salvation . . . Therefore the Blessed Virgin is invoked in the

---

6. Justin Martyr, "Dialogue with Trypho," 304–5. "[Christ] is born of the Virgin, in order that the disobedience caused by the serpent might be destroyed in the same manner in which it had originated. For Eve, an undefiled virgin, conceived the word of the serpent, and brought forth disobedience and death. But the Virgin Mary . . . gave birth to Him . . . by whom God destroys both the serpent and those angels and men who have become like the serpent."

7. Irenaeus, *Against Heresies*, 249.

8. Ibid., 410.

9. Engelsman, *The Feminine Dimension*, 132.

10. Ruether, *Mary*, 7.

11. Eugenio, *Philippine Folk Literature*, 109.

Church under the titles of Advocate, Helper, Benefactress, and Mediatrix."[12] Thomas Merton explains in a book written for novices: "Life in the Spirit is a life which [Mary] herself has obtained for us and given to us as Mediatrix of all grace."[13]

Although the elevation of Mary to semi-divine status has enabled people throughout history to connect with and honor the feminine within God, the feminine has been located in an elevated human being rather than in the very being of God.

MARY: THE QUEEN OF MOTHERHOOD

Carl Jung, the Swiss psychiatrist whose work I will explore in the next chapter, wrote about the importance of the feminine in society and the significance of the Divine feminine. He is not concerned with a theological naming of Mary as divine, but rather a psychological need for the feminine to be more valued and less marginalized. He writes that "Mary, the blessed among women, is a friend and intercessor for sinners, which all men are. Like Sophia, she is a mediatrix who leads the way to God and assures man of immortality. Her Assumption is therefore the prototype of man's bodily resurrection. As the bride of God and Queen of Heaven she holds the place of the Old Testament Sophia."[14]

The dogma Jung refers to is the Assumption of Mary (defined by Pope Pius XII in 1950) and states that Mary, like Jesus, was assumed into heavenly glory, body and soul, at the end of her earthly life.[15] Jung considers this naming of Mary alongside Jesus as "the most important religious event since the Reformation"[16] because it gives equal worth to the masculine and feminine. He states, "One could have known for a long time that there was a deep longing in the masses for an intercessor and mediatrix who would at last take her place alongside the Holy Trinity and be received as the 'Queen of heaven and Bride at the heavenly court.' For more than a thousand years it has been taken for granted that the Mother of God dwelt there."[17] Jung's

---

12. Catholic Church, *Catechism of the Catholic Church*, 252.

13. Merton, *Basic Principles of Monastic Spirituality*. Cited in Furlong, *Merton*, 231.

14. Jung, *Answer to Job*, 43.

15. Pius XII, "Munificentissimus," 44.

16. Jung, *Answer to Job*, 133.

17. Ibid., 131.

psychological perception identifies the deep human need for the feminine to be present in God.

While Jung is responding to the elevation of Mary as important from a psychological point of view, Edward Schillebeeckx, a leading modern theologian, explains from a theological perspective how Mary is the mother of all. He emphasizes that Mary, being the mother of Jesus, who is redeemer of all humanity, is thus not only mother of all, but also a partner in redemption to all: "She is also, by reason of her freely accepted motherhood with regard to Christ, who is, by his vocation, the head of the whole of mankind, fundamentally the mother of the whole of redeemed mankind. She is, moreover, not only the mother of all Christians, but also the mother of all who are not yet members of the Christian Church. She is the mother of every apostolate and every mission. She is the mother of all men because she was a partner on the objective work of redemption which applies to all men."[18]

Later chapters will explore some of the literary figures that represent the feminine Divine, but I will draw here on a prayer to Mary from Goethe's *Faust*, an interpretation of an ancient German legend, in order to convey how Mary was seen as "Goddess." In the oldest versions of this legend, Faust makes a pact with the devil, which results in his eternal damnation. Yet in the second part of Goethe's version, which was published posthumously in 1832, Faust is redeemed through the intercession of his beloved Helena and of Mary, the mother of Jesus. Faust's prayer reflects Mary's status as both the virgin Queen of Motherhood and Goddess:

> O contrite hearts, seek with your eyes
> The visage of salvation;
> Blissful in that gaze, arise,
> Through glad regeneration.
> Now may every pulse of good
> Seek to serve before thy face,
> Virgin, Queen of Motherhood,
> Keep us, Goddess, in thy grace.[19]

This one example reflects the practice of men, in different contexts and ages, praying to Mary. Of course, such shifts are very complex, and throughout the centuries, men and women have sought to relate to the feminine in many different ways. Yet the Catholic acceptance of Mary as

18. Schillebeeckx, *Mary,* 112.

19. Goethe, *Faust,* 266.

the Queen of Motherhood reveals one particular expression of how the human relationship with the Divine feminine has shifted over time.

THE FEMININE AS CHURCH

Along with the representation of Mary as the feminine Divine, a few hundred years after Christ, the Church also began to take on a feminine visage and to be portrayed as the mother and comforter of all. For example, Clement of Alexandria (d. AD 215) writes, "The male is Christ, the female is the Church. And the Books and the Apostles *plainly declare* that the Church is not of the present, but from the beginning."[20] Similarly, St. Ambrose (d. AD 397), the former governor of Aemilia-Liguria who became bishop of Milan, writes: "the Church has oil, with which she tends the wounds of her children, that the wound may not harden and spread deep. She pours the same grace not only upon the rich and mighty, but also upon men of low estate, she weighs them all in an equal balance, gathers them all into the same bosom, cherishes them in the same lap."[21] Yet as we saw with the elevation of Mary to divine status, this rendering of the Church as feminine places a more masculine focus on God, who comes to be identified as Father once the church is identified as the Mother of all.

MARY: QUEEN OF HEAVEN

In chapter 7, I will explore Thomas Merton's relationship to the feminine Divine more fully, but in this section, I will illustrate his Catholic understanding of and love for Mary. In contrast, since the Reformation, the Protestant church has emphasized Mary's humanness, withdrawing adoration from her, and criticizing the Catholic Church for their "misplaced" worship of her.

After a day in the fields of Gethsemani, the monastery in Kentucky where Thomas Merton lived for most of his adult life, he writes about how you "get in your place in the long file, and start swinging homeward along the road with your boots ringing on the asphalt and deep, deep peace in

---

20. Clement, *"The Second Epistle of Clement,"* 424, (emphasis in original).
21. Ambrose, "Letter 41: The Synagogue at Callinicum," 46.

your heart! And on your lips, silently, over and over again, the name of the Queen of Heaven, the Queen also of this valley."[22]

While novice master at Gethsemani, Thomas Merton explained the meaning of Mary in his *Basic Principles of Monastic Spirituality*: "Hence to live 'in the spirit' is in effect to live in and by Mary, the Bride of the Holy Spirit . . . To acknowledge Mary perfectly as our Queen is then to abandon ourselves entirely to the action of the Holy Spirit, who comes to us through her."[23] Later, in his best-selling *New Seeds of Contemplation*, he writes that to "love her and to know her is to discover the true meaning of everything and to have access to all wisdom. Without her, the knowledge of Christ is only speculation. But in her it becomes experience because all the humility and poverty, without which Christ cannot be known, were given to her."[24] For the Catholic, he explains that "The genuine significance of Catholic devotion to Mary is to be seen in the light of the Incarnation itself. The Church cannot separate the Son from the Mother."[25] We see his love for Mary and his recognition of the importance of her place in our responding to God when he writes: "And it is necessary that the world should acknowledge her and that the praise of God's great work in her should be sung in poetry and that cathedrals should be built in her name. For unless Our Lady is recognized as the Mother of God and as the Queen of all the saints and angels and as the hope of the world, faith in God will remain incomplete."[26]

In his autobiography *The Seven Storey Mountain*, Merton writes about his sense that Mary was caring for him even when he was oblivious of God. He speaks to Mary in prayer as if speaking to the God who plans ahead, who sees the future, who cares for the wayward. When writing of leaving England, he says in a prayer to Mary:

> I was not sure where I was going and I could not see what I would do when I got to New York. But you saw further and clearer than I and you opened the seas before my ship whose track led me across the waters to a place I had never dreamed of, and which you were even then preparing for me to be my rescue and my shelter and my home. And when I thought there was no God and no love and no mercy, you were leading me all the while into the midst

22. Merton, *Elected Silence*, 347.
23. Merton, *Basic Principles of Monastic Spirituality*. Cited in Furlong, *Merton*, 231.
24. Merton, *New Seeds of Contemplation*, 168.
25. Ibid., 71.
26. Ibid., 174.

of His love and His mercy and taking me, without my knowing anything about it, to the house that would hide me in the secret of His face.[27]

He also prays to Mary for other lost souls, calling her the Holy Queen of Souls and Refuge of Sinners. Such names reflect Merton's belief in Mary's Divinity. He writes:

Glorious Mother of God, shall I ever again distrust you or your God before Whose throne you are irresistible in your intercession? Shall I ever turn my eyes from your hands, from your face, or from your eyes? Shall I ever look anywhere else but in the face of your love to find our true counsel and to know my way in all these days and all the moments of my life? As you have dealt with me, Lady, deal also with all my millions of brothers and sisters who live in the same misery that I knew then. Lead them in spite of themselves and guide them by your tremendous influence, O Holy Queen of Souls and Refuge of Sinners.[28]

During Merton's early years in America, his spirituality blossomed and he began to desire to be a priest. On holiday in Cuba during Lent in 1940, his bus came through the valley to the Caribbean Sea, and the yellow basilica of Our Lady of Cobre came into sight, prompting him to pray to Mary: "You will ask Christ to make me His priest and I will give you my heart, Lady. And if you will obtain for me this priesthood, I will remember you at my first Mass in such a way that the Mass will be for you and offered through your hands in gratitude to the Holy Trinity Who has used your love to win me this great grace."[29]

Throughout his journals, which were written through his life as a monk and hermit, Merton revealed his intimate relationship with Mary, to whom he prayed in the same way that he prayed to God, trusting in her care for him. Over time, he began to merge his ideas about Mary with Wisdom, Sophia, though he continued to pray to Mary. In March 1966, two years before his death, he wrote in his journal: "Mary ever Virgin, Mother of God our Savior, I entrust myself entirely to your loving intercession and care because you are my Mother and I am your dear child, full of trouble, conflict, error, confusion, and prone to sin. My whole life must change, but

27. Merton, *The Seven Storey Mountain*, 129–30.
28. Ibid., 130.
29. Ibid., 282.

because I can do nothing to change it by my own powers, I entrust it with all my needs and cares to you."[30]

Thomas Merton's great veneration of and love for Mary reflects his deep sense of her care for him. While some Protestants may think such prayers would be better directed to God, his writing reflects an openness to the feminine that blossoms into a deeper relationship with God.

CONCLUSION

As we have seen in this chapter, Merton and other writers have found salvation through the Divine feminine in Mary. Many others have discovered the Divine feminine in the God of the Bible. This search reflects the human longing for love and care, knowing and being known by One who is both masculine and feminine, immanent and transcendent, self-revealing and yet also mystery beyond our knowing. Throughout the Christian tradition, we can find examples of men and women who have sought and found the Divine feminine. In part II, we will turn to that search as it has been revealed by contemporary writers.

---

30. Merton, *Learning to Love*, 360.

5

The Inner Cathedral
Mapping the Journey of Differentiation and Integration

He whose desire turns away from the outer things, reaches the place of the soul. If he does not find the soul, the horror of emptiness will overcome him, and fear will drive him with a whip lashing time and again in a desperate endeavor and a blind desire for the hollow things of the world. He becomes a fool through his endless desire, and forgets the way of his soul, never to find her again. He will run after all things, and will seize hold of them, but he will not find his soul, since he would find her only in himself.[1]

JUNG'S EARLY JOURNEY

Carl Jung (1875–1961) was born in Switzerland to a father who was a Protestant Reformed pastor and a mother who had six brothers who were clergymen. "He had throughout his life an absorbing interest in religion,"[2] and as a boy felt himself to be "in a state of communion with

1. Jung and Shamdasani, *The Red Book,* 129.
2. Bryant, *Jung and the Christian Way,* 1.

nature and the cosmos. He inhabited 'God's world.'"[3] In later life he wrote, "I find that all my thoughts circle round God, like the planets round the sun, and are irresistibly attracted by him. I would feel it to be the grossest sin if I were to oppose any resistance to this force."[4]

He felt himself to have two alternating personalities: the school boy who read novels, and the other who "pursued religious reflections in solitude . . . This personality felt most real."[5] The young Carl did not identify with the religion of his father, which he found too rigid and legalistic and lacking in life. Yet he felt a direct and immediate experience of the living God,[6] which remained important to him throughout his life. When it became time to choose a career, his two personalities were in conflict—one wanting to pursue the sciences and the other the humanities. He chose the sciences and eventually psychiatry, which "represented a fusion of the interests of his two personalities."[7]

Jung married in his mid-twenties and had five children. He practiced psychiatry, but became more and more "disenchanted by the limitations of experimental and statistical methods."[8] In 1906, in his early thirties, he began a correspondence with Freud. This correspondence has sparked a widespread misunderstanding that Freud and his psychoanalysis were the principal source for Jung's work. Yet Jung protested that his own scientific theories had been developed before he met Freud.[9]

In 1908, Jung had a house built on the shore of Lake Zurich and remained there for the rest of his life, devoting himself to his own practice and research interests in mythology, folklore, and religion. He found the mythological work "exciting and intoxicating."[10] A few years later, he began his "most difficult experiment."[11]

3. Shamdasani, "Introduction," *The Red Book*, 5.

4. Jung, *Memories, Dreams and Reflections*, xi.

5. Shamdasani, "Introduction," *The Red Book*, 5.

6. Ibid., 5.

7. Ibid., 8.

8. Ibid., 11.

9. Ibid.

10. Ibid., 12.

11. Ibid., 24. "In December 1913 he referred to the first of the *Black Books* as the 'book of my most difficult experiment.'"

JUNG'S MIDLIFE: "THE DIFFICULT EXPERIMENT"

Beginning in 1913, when Jung was in his late-thirties, he began experimenting with the active imagination. He would enter a fantasy and experience it as though it were real, actively responding to the elements within it, and later reflecting on the experience in order to gain understanding. A few years before his death, Jung wrote: "The years of which I have spoken to you, when I pursued the inner images, were the most important time of my life. Everything else is to be derived from this . . . the numinous beginning, which contained everything, was then."[12] Clearly, this process had profound significance for Jung. During this midlife journey, he engaged specifically with his own soul, which he identified as feminine. At first, he resisted this interpretation, but later he began to teach about the necessity to engage with one's soul through the opposite gender: the feminine anima for men, the masculine animus for women.

Jung wrote his reflections in what he eventually called his *Black Books*. "I said to myself, 'What is this I am doing, it certainly is not science, what is it?' Then a voice said to me, 'That is art.' This made the strangest sort of impression on me . . . I don't know why exactly, but I knew to a certainty that the voice that had said my writing was art had come from a woman . . . Well I said emphatically to this voice that what I was doing was not art, and I felt a great resistance grow up within me."[13] Jung explains: "'In putting down all this material for analysis, I was in effect writing letters to my anima, that is part of myself with a different viewpoint from my own.'"[14]

Through personal experiences, active imagination, conversations with his soul, and written reflections, Jung came to understand the necessity for integrating the different parts of himself, especially the soul—the anima, or the feminine within. Later, he explained how to have these conversations with the soul, where one would begin with a feeling, or an affect, and then allow it to speak:

> Starting from the fact that in a state of affect one often surrenders involuntarily to the truths of the other side, would it not be far better to make use of an affect so as to give the other side an opportunity to speak? It could therefore be said just as truly that one should cultivate the art of conversing with oneself in the setting

12. Ibid., vii.
13. Ibid., 21.
14. Ibid.

provided by an affect, as though the affect itself were speaking without regard to our rational criticism. So long as the affect is speaking, criticism must be withheld.[15]

His *Black Books* (and later *The Red Book*) comprise many conversations that reveal his unfolding journey. For example, he writes: "But my soul said to me, 'Do you think little of yourself?' I do not believe so. My soul answered, 'Then listen, do you think little of me? Do you still not know that you are not writing a book to feed your vanity, but that you are speaking with me?'"[16] And again: "This life is the way, the long sought-after way to the unfathomable, which we call divine. There is no other way, all other ways are false paths. I found the right way, it led me to you, to my soul."[17] He notes that he had to be "forced" to speak to his soul, "to call upon her as a living and self-existing being. I had to become aware that I had lost my soul."[18]

In this mid-life journey, Jung is very conscious that he could seek after "the hollow things of the world," but he recognizes that if he is to become fully mature, he needs to let go these outer things and find the inner way. He observes:

> He whose desire turns away from the outer things reaches the place of the soul. If he does not find the soul, the horror of emptiness will overcome him, and fear will drive him with a whip lashing time and again in a desperate endeavor and a blind desire for the hollow things of the world. He becomes a fool through his endless desire, and forgets the way of his soul, never to find her again. He will run after all things, and will seize hold of them, but he will not find his soul, since he would find her only in himself.[19]

He continues: "My friends it is wise to nourish the soul, otherwise you will breed dragons and devils in your heart."[20]

Cary Baynes, who worked with Jung for a time, comments about this passage: "I came to your conversation with your soul . . . It is no cry of the young man awakening into life but that of the mature man who has lived fully and richly in ways of the world and yet knows almost abruptly, one

15. Jung, "Aspects of the Feminine," 91.
16. Jung and Shamdasani, *The Red Book*, 145.
17. Jung and Shamdasani, *The Red Book,* 128.
18. Ibid., 129.
19. Ibid.
20. Ibid., 130.

might say, that he has missed the essence. The vision came at the height of your power, when you could have gone on just as you were with perfect worldly success."[21] Jung himself later described his personal transformation at this time as an example of the beginning of the second half of life, which is marked by a return to the soul after the goals and ambitions of the first half of life have been achieved.

JUNG'S JOURNEY OF INTEGRATION: *ANIMA* AND GOD

For Jung, this second half of life was marked by the challenge to integrate the feminine into his self. His studies in mythology revealed many stories that traced the significance of the masculine journey and interaction with the feminine. He writes: "This demon-woman of mythology is in truth 'the sister-wife-mother,' the woman in the man, who unexpectedly turns up during the second half of life and tries to effect a forcible change of personality."[22] Jung came to recognize the "woman in the man"—or the anima, the soul—as a part of the man that has been repressed or ignored. His difficult experiment of active imagination led him to engage with his soul as an autonomous being in order to recognize it more clearly and to integrate it more consciously.

Prior to this second half of his journey, Jung realized that he sought the good of his soul outside of himself. His words echo Augustine's: "For behold Thou wert within me, and I outside; and I sought Thee outside,"[23] which recognize the invitation to seek God within oneself. Jung writes:

> On the second night I called out to my soul: "I am weary my soul, my wandering has lasted too long, my search for myself outside of myself. Now I have gone through events and find you behind all of them. For I made discoveries on my erring through events, humanity, and the world. I found men. And you, my soul, I found again, first in images within men and then you yourself. I found you where I least expected you. You climbed out of a dark shaft. You announced yourself to me in advance in dreams . . . Who are you, child? My dreams have represented you as a child and as a maiden."[24]

21. Ibid., 130, n. 44.

22. Jung, *Symbols of Transformation*, 362.

23. Augustine, *The Confessions of Saint Augustine*, 188.

24. Jung and Shamdasani, *The Red Book*, 130–31.

This search to respond to the soul led Jung to his inner feminine self and also to God: "I am ignorant of your mystery. Forgive me if I speak as in a dream, like a drunkard—are you God? . . . I had to recognize and accept that my soul is a child and that my God in my soul is a child. *If you are boys, your God is a woman. If you are women, your God is a boy. If you are men, your God is a maiden. The God is where you are not.*"[25] Moreover, he interpreted his patients' feelings of emptiness or senselessness as religious crises, which could be treated with therapy. He observes, "Many neuroses are caused primarily by the fact that people blind themselves to their own religious promptings because of a childish passion for rational enlightenment."[26]

This intense pilgrimage of reflection prompted Jung to conceive of the anima within the man and the animus within the woman. He described the integration of the anima as a spiritual journey, which was essential to the development of the self. He referred to this process of interacting with and integrating the feminine within as differentiation. Jung's conceptualization of the spiritual journey of integration prompted his shift from bonding with the mother to the greater mother, whom he recognized in "the goddess, and especially the Mother of God, the Virgin, and Sophia."[27]

Jung explains that the boy's relationship with the mother is a necessary and important part of the grounding of his life: "The mother is the first feminine being with whom the man-to-be comes in contact, and she cannot help playing, overtly or covertly, consciously or unconsciously, upon the son's masculinity, just as the son in his turn grows increasingly aware of his mother's femininity, or unconsciously responds to it by instinct."[28] The boy's relationship with his mother develops within him what Jung describes as feminine attributes:

> This gives him a great capacity for friendship, which often creates ties of astonishing tenderness between men and may even rescue friendship between the sexes from the limbo of the impossible. He may have good taste and an aesthetic sense which are fostered by the presence of the feminine streak. Then he may be supremely gifted as a teacher because of his almost feminine insight and tact. He is likely to have a feeling for history, and to be conservative

---

25. Ibid., 131, 135 (italics in original).
26. Jung, *The Practice of Psychotherapy*, 46.
27. Jung, "Archetypes and the Collective Unconscious," 81.
28. Ibid., 85–86.

in the best sense and cherish the values of the past. Often he is endowed with a wealth of religious feelings, which help to bring the *ecclesia spiritualis* into reality; and a spiritual receptivity which makes him responsive to revelation.[29]

Though Jung values these feminine attributes, he finds it unhealthy to project these attributes onto the mother (as if she were a goddess rather than human) or onto another woman. He recognizes that it is common to do so during the first half of life, but observes that as a man matures, he will need to identify these attributes within himself. He writes that the task is to "dissolve the projections, in order to restore their contents to the individual who has involuntarily lost them by projecting them outside himself."[30]

Yet the concept of the "inner feminine" was not original to Jung, who searched literature and myths to help him understand human longing and selfhood. In earlier centuries, many writers described their souls as feminine in poetry and religious allegory. In the fourteenth century, Dante writes of Beatrice, a feminine soul who guides him through heaven. Jung explains: "Dante is the spiritual knight of his lady; for her sake he embarks on the adventure of the lower and upper worlds. In this heroic endeavor her image is exalted into the heavenly, mystical figure of the mother of God—a figure that has detached itself from the object and become the personification of a purely psychological factor, or rather, of those unconscious contents whose personification I have termed the *anima*."[31] And as I describe in chapter 4, Goethe draws on the Greek myth of Helen of Troy to describe Faust's longing for Helena and the "eternal feminine" as salvation for Faust's own soul.

By personifying the soul as the inner feminine, writers symbolically describe the mystery of communion with God or marriage with Christ.[32] For example, in the *Holy Sonnets*, John Donne draws on the symbolism of the feminine soul crying out to God to rescue and betroth himself to her. "Take me to you, imprison me, for I, Except you enthral me, never shall be free, Nor ever chaste except you ravish me."[33] Jung suggests that this identification with one's own soul as feminine is also evident in St. John's "Dark

29. Ibid., 86–87.

30. Ibid., 84.

31. Jung, "Aspects of the Feminine," 5.

32. Johnson, *Inner Work,* 30

33. Donne, *Holy Sonnets,* 30.

Night": "O night that has united the Lover with his beloved, transforming the beloved in her Lover."[34]

Jung acknowledges these cultural personifications of the feminine and observes that such archetypes will become significant "only when one patiently tries to discover why and in what fashion they are meaningful to a living individual."[35] The inner feminine energizes men towards relationship, calling them to relate to their own souls—and thereby into deeper relationality with God. Thus Jung maps out the journey of differentiation and the integration of the whole person.

DIVINE ROMANCE: THE JOURNEY OF INTEGRATION

As discussed above, we learn about the feminine through early bonding with our mothers. Yet when a boy learns that what is named as "feminine" is unacceptable in a young man, he will project those feminine parts of himself on to the "other," or woman. Unless he is prepared to do the inner work of integration, he will continue to project the unrecognized parts of himself onto other people. Sometimes, he will project parts of himself that he does not like onto others, and then he will hate or criticize them. Sometimes, he will project parts of himself that he does like—yet which he may not be able to acknowledge—onto others, and then he will fall in love with them.

Thus whenever we react inappropriately to others, there is likely something within us that needs to be acknowledged and integrated. Few young people have integrated the masculine and feminine within themselves. They are still wrestling with what it means to be a man or a woman, expressing only one dimension of their inner complex selves. When someone of the opposite sex expresses qualities not yet flowering within themselves, falling in love is almost inevitable. "When we are 'in love' we believe we have found the ultimate meaning in life, revealed in another human being. We feel we are finally completed."[36] Or, more dramatically, "we fall in love against our will. Our hearts suddenly go off on crazy paths of their own, leaving our cool, collected minds aghast and struggling vainly to maintain order and

---

34. Kavanagh and Rodriguez, *Collected Works of St. John of the Cross,* 358.

35. Jung, *Man and his Symbols,* 88.

36. Johnson, *We,* xii.

dignity."[37] Nevertheless, if we understand falling in love within the context of the spiritual journey, "being in love is a deeply religious experience."[38]

Robert Johnson, a Christian interpreter of Jung, examines the romantic images of our culture in his book *We: Understanding the Psychology of Romantic Love.* Johnson shows that for centuries we have used romantic love to replace the spiritual journey of tending the inner work of integration. "Rather than look within himself where anima natively dwells he demands his soul of his external environment; he demands it of woman."[39]

Johnson uses the thousand-year-old story of the romance of Tristan and Iseult (or Isolde) to demonstrate how our Western culture has become enamored with romantic longing as a replacement for the inner work and the spiritual journey. The myth of Tristan and Iseult dates from around the twelfth century. The Grail myths of this time recount the adventures of noble knights who slay dragons and fulfill conquests, proving their loyalty to their king and often a lady. Typically, the knight's relationship to the lady is not romantic or sexual, but rather marked by loyal devotion and service. Beginning with the myth of Tristan and Iseult, however, the romance shifts from a lyrical story to a romantic story as we now understand it: the noble knight serves his queen and they fall in love. Tristan and Iseult's love for each other becomes worship, for they each believe that only the other can give them life and that death is better than life without the beloved. In our Western culture, we have inherited this inner belief about seeking earthly, romantic fulfillment of an ideal love rather than tracing a spiritual journey of longing for the Divine.

Jung identifies the man's essential spiritual journey as withdrawing these projections from others and cultivating wholeness within. Following Jung, Johnson argues that if a man's intimate marriage relationship is going to last, he will need to address this inner work. He writes: "the principle work is to be done within the individual him/herself,[40] and to learn to cope with one's own masculinity and femininity within is an absolute prerequisite before one has the right to talk about exterior relationships. A man will treat a woman almost exactly the way he treats his own interior feminine. In fact, he hasn't the ability to see a woman, objectively speaking,

37. Johnson, *Inner Work,* 129.

38. Johnson, *Inner Gold,* 18.

39. Johnson, *We,* 66.

40. Johnson explores the contrasting journeys of men and women in *He: Understanding Masculine Psychology; She: Understanding Feminine Psychology.*

until he has made some kind of peace with his interior woman."[41] If a man can withdraw his expectations that the woman will fulfill his longing for relatedness and learn to value the "feminine" within himself, then "Anima [will be] returned to the inner kingdom; feminine and masculine [will be] joined; the self [will be] completed and made whole."[42]

RICHARD ROHR'S JOURNEY TOWARDS UNION WITH GOD

Along with Robert Johnson, several other writers who explore the male journey have been influenced by Jung. In *The Wild Man's Journey: Reflections on Male Spirituality*, Franciscan writer and speaker Richard Rohr explores the integration of the masculine and the feminine in order to come to a deeper knowing of God. In describing the relationship between God and gender, he writes:

> I believe that God is the ultimate combination of whatever it means to be male and whatever it means to be female. God is fully sexual in the deepest meaning of that term. It is obvious to me that we must, therefore, find public ways to recognize, honor, and name the feminine nature of God, since we have overly limited our metaphors for God for centuries . . . all those wonderful sexually charged words for God—such as Mother, Father, Son, Daughter, Bride, Bridegroom, Friend, Guest Lover, Jealous Lover or even Seducer.[43]

Speaking of the New Jerusalem community that he founded in 1971, he writes: "As a group the spiritual task confronting us was to move from the common masculine and into the feminine side of our nature . . . to develop the feminine virtues of listening, empathy, dialogue and trust that are so needed in community."[44] He identifies the masculine as "self-possession, detachment and free decisions for and against. It has to do with outer over inner, action over more reflection, and a love of things, events and history itself over more concern for subjective states and feelings."[45] But then he names "masculinity at its best" as a more integrated whole: "Love for the

41. From an interview with Robert Johnson and Lila Forest, *In Context,* 19.

42. Johnson, *We,* 92.

43. Rohr, *Adam's Return,* xiii–xiv.

44. Rohr and Martos, *The Wild Man's Journey,* 2.

45. Ibid., 149.

whole, for the big picture and the entire narrative. It is self-sacrificing love over mere attachment or codependent small relationship. Finally, it is being quite comfortable with power, precisely because one has walked through powerlessness—and emerged unashamed."[46] And he adds, "Unless the man is reintegrated into the ordinary world of family, love and loyalties, he is not a hero at all."[47]

Rohr moves away from Jung's emphasis on "integrating the feminine" to focus on the first and second halves of life. He draws on archetypes such as the warrior, the king, the lover, and the wise man, noting that most non-Western cultures have rites of initiation that mark the journey into adulthood. In *Adam's Return*, Rohr delineates the dimensions of what a young man learns through initiation and then through his life: life is hard, you are not that important, life is not about you, you are not in control, and you are going to die.[48] Because of men's more dominant position in many cultures, they typically need to be taught these lessons more explicitly. By way of contrast, in most cultures, women learn these lessons as a natural part of their life journey because they are "historically initiated by their one-down position in patriarchal societies, by the humiliations of blood (menstruation, labor, and menopause), by the ego-decentralizing role of child raising, and by their greater investment in relationships."[49]

Thus in more recent years, Rohr has been teaching about the life journey through a multiplicity of images and archetypes. He comments that in his earlier years, he talked a lot about "men getting in touch with their feminine, and women getting in touch with their masculine."[50] He continues, "We build on that, we agree with that, but . . . that's too easy. You can all do that in your private inner world. It oft times has little to do with social, political, mystical, radical level, it's all just something I can think about."[51] Rohr recognizes that it is too easy for us to stay in our minds and not make changes in the outer world—the social world of real relationships. Our more profound journey is union with God, and Rohr identifies sexuality and spirituality as two gates into this same temple.[52] He acknowledges that

46. Ibid.

47. Ibid., 153.

48. Rohr, *Adam's Return*, 32–33.

49. Ibid., 7–8.

50. Bourgeault and Rohr, *God As Us!*, CD.

51. Ibid.

52. Rohr, *Gates of the Temple*, CD.

the journey for men and women usually has a different starting point, but union with God is the ultimate aim. *"The object and goal of all spirituality is finally the same for all genders: union, divine love, inner aliveness, soul abundance, generous service to the neighbor and the world.* In these essentials and in the Great Whole 'there is no distinction . . . between male and female' (Galatians 3:28)."[53]

JAMES NELSON'S MASCULINE JOURNEY: ACTIVE AND RECEPTIVE

James B. Nelson also explores Christian male spirituality in *The Intimate Connection: Male Sexuality, Masculine Spirituality.*[54] Nelson recognizes that "integrating the feminine" may not be a helpful image for some men, and he finds Jung's bifurcation of the masculine and feminine stereotypical and unhelpful.[55] Instead, he traces the male journey from his childhood dependence on the mother to a more independent sense of self and masculinity. He recognizes the importance of both the mothering and the fathering role, but acknowledges that the boy often pulls away from intimacy with the nurturing mother as a way to find his own maleness. "Intimacy now becomes a threat to the male's struggle for masculine identity. The very thing he craves, the thing all persons need for nourishing life itself, is a problem. He has established his tenuous hold on masculinity through separation and boundary-making, and emotional closeness threatens that precarious grip."[56]

The way the father relates to his son during this process is crucial. If the father is distant, or if he only shows love or affirmation when his son performs, the maturing boy will head towards self-protection and competition instead of intimacy and vulnerability. "The emotionally and physically distant father who rewards his son with love made conditional on performance expectations contributes to a male shaped for independence but not intimacy, self-protection but not vulnerability, competition but not mutuality."[57] An active nurturing father, on the other hand, will help shape the young man for a more receptive and vulnerable spirituality.

53. Rohr, *Unitive Consciousness,* 147 (italics in the original).

54. Nelson, *The Intimate Connection.*

55. Ibid., 93.

56. Ibid., 42.

57. Ibid., 43.

Sadly, Nelson recognizes that it is more common for men to experience "a deep tension between intimacy and masculinity."[58] Thus he seeks to balance strength and energy with openness and mutuality. "There is a deep and dark, instinctual Zeus-type energy that we men want and need to tap. It seems related to the desire to penetrate and to explore the mystery of otherness, a desire important to human fulfillment. At the same time, this needs balance through the development of a more receptive and vulnerable male sexuality that will form the grounding for a more receptive and vulnerable masculine spirituality."[59]

Nelson acknowledges that for many men, the idea of "getting in touch with the feminine" means connecting with something alien, outside of themselves. Thus he steps away from this language and compares the meanings of the phallus and the penis as a way of exploring masculinity as both active and receptive. The phallus is the erect penis—strong, powerful, penetrating, and wholly masculine. But most of the time, men do not have an erection—a phallus—and so the penis is soft, used for urination, simply present. Thus the penis symbolizes another side of masculinity—present, receptive, ordinary. "The phallic energy in us is also solar: penetrating, thrusting, achieving and with the desire for self-transcendence. Equally important and *equally male,* there is good penile energy in us. It is soft, vulnerable and receptive. It knows that size is not merely quantitative, more truly it is the strength of mutuality which can be enriched by other life without losing its own center."[60]

Nelson takes the metaphor further in reflecting on orgasm and the body's experience of connection. He observes:

> The orgasmic sexual experience brings its own revelation. The hard and explosive phallic achievement becomes in an instant the soft, vulnerable tears of the penis. Both are fully male. Both are deeply grounded in a man's bodily reality. Both dimensions of life are fully present when a man is most human. And to be fully human is to know the Christ—not as supernatural invader but as that reality truest to our own natures, and as that reality which intimately connects us with everyone and everything else.[61]

58. Ibid., 42.
59. Ibid., 43.
60. Ibid., 110.
61. Ibid., 111.

In tracing the masculine journey from separation from the mother towards the discovery of the masculine as both powerful and vulnerable, Nelson reflects on the wounding effects of a masculinized God. "Yet healing that wounded god image is complex. The image has served what we thought was our self-interest. When God became male, males were divinized, and patriarchy had cosmic blessing. At the same time, we have resisted that one-sided masculinized deity, for a male God suggests to men their feminization."[62] Nelson is exploring the masculine need of a God who is both feminine and masculine, a father God who shows unconditional love and a mother God who is deeply nurturing. "We have had enough of certain kinds of fatherhood, and we want a different understanding of God. To embrace the 'feminine' in God is to embrace the promise of that deep nurturing presence and immanence that we so need."[63] Yet he also acknowledges the complexity of this process, since the feminine in the Divine "raises our unconscious anger at the mother who abandoned us and pushed us out into a man's world where the clues and expectations about our own deepest meanings were hard to find. It is all very confusing in the heart of a man's heart."[64]

Nelson offers a metaphor that weaves together the powerful and receptive aspects of a man's masculinity. He also taps into the male's unconscious need and ambivalent longing for intimacy, which remains after separating from the mother, and he recognizes how this helps to explain some men's resistance to the feminine Divine.

Both Richard Rohr and James Nelson draw on the Jungian tradition of gendered imagining and embodied sexuality, though they outline alternative understandings of the masculine journey and spirituality. Both owe their insights to Jung's emphasis on men's need to engage with their souls and to respond to the feminine Divine as they journey towards maturity and healthy relationships with people of both genders.

LOOKING AHEAD: EMERGING PATTERNS

In this chapter, I have outlined Jung's basic conceptualizations, which will have resonance for the remaining chapters of the book. In chapter 6, I will explore George MacDonald's fantasy writings, focusing on his pattern of

62. Ibid., 45.

63. Ibid.

64. Ibid., 45.

representing both the romantic and the spiritual with feminine figures. In Jung's terms, MacDonald's characters clearly engage with the soul and come to discover the feminine within themselves as they journey towards wholeness. In chapter 7, I will explore the life of Thomas Merton, who (like MacDonald) lost his mother as a child and withdrew from the feminine for a long period of his life. In Jungian terms, Merton journeyed towards wholeness and completion by rediscovering the feminine both internally and externally—in God, himself, and others. In chapter 8, I will examine Paul Young's representation of God as a black woman in *The Shack* and as female in *Cross Roads*. I also trace the author's life journey towards imaging God as female, which echoes the Jungian analysis. For both Merton and Young, their love affairs were part of their journey towards wholeness in God. As Johnson summarizes: "we must take our soul out of romantic love and return it to an inner place—the inner cathedral."[65] In chapter 9, I will explore the experiences of men in this century who are discovering the feminine Divine. Each of these chapters explores the lives and writings of men who returned to that inner cathedral in the search for wholeness and deeper union with the fullness of God—who is male and female, mother and father, lover and friend.

65. Johnson, *We*, 181.

6

Eyes Forever Young
George MacDonald

. . . a woman-face, the most wonderful, I thought, that I had ever beheld. For it was older than any countenance I had ever looked upon . . . but . . . her eyes . . . were absolutely young—those of a woman of five-and-twenty . . . the eyes were very incarnations of soft light . . . A wondrous sense of refuge and repose came upon me. I felt like a boy who has got home from school, miles across the hills, through a heavy storm of wind and snow.[1]

EARLY LIFE

George MacDonald (1824—1905) published over twenty novels—some for children, some for adults, and, most importantly, those "for the childlike, whether of five, or fifty, or seventy-five."[2] His stories, which explore the ideal and the shadow, good and evil, inspired the fantasies of C. S. Lewis and J. R. R. Tolkien. When he was in his twenties, he wrote his first book, *Within and Without,* a long verse drama about a monk who leaves the

---

1. MacDonald, *Phantastes,* 202–3.
2. MacDonald, "The Fantastic Imagination," 317.

monastery to seek God.[3] Throughout his life, he explored this relationship between spirituality and writing—the human journey and the search for expression. C. S. Lewis said of MacDonald's novels that they were more useful as theology than fiction.[4] Yet MacDonald is largely considered to be the "father of fantasy" literature.[5] In *George MacDonald: An Anthology*, C. S. Lewis states, "I know hardly any other writer who seems closer, or more continually close, to the Spirit of Christ himself."[6]

When MacDonald was eight years old, his mother died of tuberculosis. Upon her death, his paternal grandmother took a major role in his life. "She represents one major pole in his religious education, that of a more rigid Federal Calvinism reinforced by his Church, the predominant culture, and his primary school teacher."[7] This strict legalism became a counterpoint for the rest of his life. When he was fourteen, his father remarried, and although George was fond of his step-mother, "the most important relationship in his life was with his father, whom he loved and respected."[8] "From his own father, he said, he first learned that Fatherhood must be at the core of the universe."[9]

After initially studying chemistry at university, MacDonald turned to theology. At twenty-six, he became the pastor of a Congregational church in England, but his heterodox beliefs were not accepted by his congregation. Rebelling against the harsh Calvinism of his childhood, his theology was close to universalism, and he was much more concerned with practice than doctrine. "He hated the way that people could be 'religious', or 'churchgoing', yet fail to show any real sign of being Christ's disciples."[10] He remained a pastor for only two years. His poor health forced him to move with his wife and family to a healthier climate, and his congregation's rejection caused him to turn to writing.

3. Page, "Introduction" in *Phantastes*, 11–12.

4. Ibid., 26.

5. MacDonald, *Lilith*, 241.

6. Lewis, *George MacDonald*, 18.

7. Dearborn, *Baptized Imagination*, 10.

8. Page, "Introduction" in *Phantastes*, 8.

9. Lewis, *George MacDonald*, 10.

10. Page, "Introduction" in *Phantastes*, 13.

SEARCHING FOR THE DIVINE FEMININE

MacDonald's early loss of his mother and his rejection of the harsh, all-powerful God of his rigid Calvinist upbringing opened him to encounters with the Divine feminine. Through stories and poems, MacDonald found a way to explore the feminine in God without raising intellectual objections.

By writing fantasy stories, MacDonald sought to express ideas that would appeal to readers' hearts rather than intellectually convince their minds. He wanted to awaken the truth deep within, thus inspiring readers towards transformation. He explains: "A fairy-tale, a sonata, a gathering storm, a limitless night, seizes you and sweeps you away: do you begin at once to wrestle with it and ask whence its power over you, whither it is carrying you? . . . The greatest forces lie in the region of the uncomprehended . . . The best thing you can do for your fellow, next to rousing his conscience, is—not to give him things to think about, but to wake things up that are in him."[11] He says that he uses imagery to communicate truth because "beauty is the only stuff in which Truth can be clothed; and you may, if you will, call Imagination the tailor that cuts her garments to fit her."[12] In describing the power of the fantastic imagination, he writes, "A fairytale, like a butterfly or bee, helps itself on all sides, sips at every wholesome flower, and spoils not one."[13]

Through stories and fairy-tales, MacDonald woos the reader into a closer relationship with God. As David Neuhouser comments, "Perhaps the theme MacDonald emphasized most in his [theological] writings was that of God as a loving father. However, in his fairy tales God is portrayed as a loving mother."[14] Thus it should be no surprise that he uses feminine figures to image the Divine given his understanding that "there is no type so near the highest idea of relation to a God, as that of the child to his mother. Her face is God, her bosom Nature, her arms are Providence—all love—one love—to him an undivided bliss."[15]

An early example of the Divine feminine appears in MacDonald's poem "A Hidden Life," which was written when in his twenties:

A mighty woman sat, with waiting face.

11. MacDonald, "The Fantastic Imagination," 279.

12. Ibid., 277.

13. Ibid., 278.

14. Neuhouser, "God as *Mother*," 42–4.

15. MacDonald, *A Dish of Orts*, 44.

Calm as that life whose rapt intensity
Borders on death, silent, waiting for him,

To make him grand forever with a kiss.[16]

The mighty woman is the Divine feminine whose deep intent is to give life, to draw each person into the fullness of the life nascent within. In MacDonald's writing, kisses—along with songs and stories—give life, healing and even rebirth. Thus the metaphor of the ever-present feminine who births and brings forth life is woven throughout MacDonald's writing.

LONGING FOR THE FEMININE DIVINE: *PHANTASTES*

MacDonald wrote *Phantastes: A Faerie Romance for Men and Women* during a seven-week period in his early thirties. The novel, which he wrote for adults, traces the longing for the Divine Other—the feminine—by following the hero, Anados, on his journey through Fairy Land. Anados, which means "upwards" or "pathless," is used by Plato to describe the pathway from the physical self to a higher plane of reality.[17]

At the beginning of *Phantastes*, twenty-one-year-old Anados encounters a tiny fairy figure who seems a mix of the romantic ideal and the Divine feminine. After taking on human size to engage with him, "she stood a tall, gracious lady, with pale face and large blue eyes. Her dark hair flowed behind, wavy but uncurled, down to her waist, and against it her form stood clear in its robe of white . . . Overcome with the presence of beauty which I could now perceive, and drawn towards her by an attraction irresistible as incomprehensible, I suppose I stretched out my arms towards her, for she drew back a step or two."[18] Then the fairy woman tells Anados that she will grant him his wish to enter the fairy country. "'You will find the way into Fairy Land tomorrow. Now look into my eyes.' Eagerly I did so. They filled me with an unknown longing. I remembered somehow that my mother

---

16. MacDonald, *A Hidden Life*, 36.

17. MacDonald, *Phantastes*, 44. Plato's famous allegory of the cave begins with people chained to a cave wall, who perceive life by the shadows projected onto the wall in front of them. As they grow in freedom, they eventually leave the cave and view reality directly.

18. Ibid., 44–45.

died when I was a baby. I looked deeper and deeper, till they spread around me like seas, and I sank in their waters."[19]

On Anados' first night in Fairy Land, he is rescued from danger by the spirit of the beech tree, a woman who "kissed me with the sweetest kiss of winds and odours. There was a cool faithfulness in the kiss that revived my heart wonderfully. I felt that I feared . . . no more." She then makes him a talisman to keep him from danger, "singing a strange, sweet song, which I could not understand, but which left in me a feeling like this—'I saw thee ne'er before, I see thee never more; but love, and help, and pain, beautiful one, have made thee mine, till all my years are done.'"[20]

Throughout the story, more beautiful young female figures appear, but they are all elusive and unattainable, though Anados continues to seek and long for them. The only exceptions are those who are evil and want to entrap him. The beautiful young women symbolically represent the romantic ideal, and as Anados journeys through Fairy Land, he confronts his selfish, grasping desire—his shadow—as he longs to discover his more altruistic, spiritual self.

Early on, Anados discovers the White Lady, a figure encrusted in marble. He tries to free her with his knife and discovers "a reposing woman. She lay on one side, with her hand under her cheek, and her face towards me; but her hair had fallen partly over her face, so that I could not see the expression of the whole."[21] Typically, MacDonald pictures the romantic ideal as mysterious, only partially known and yet awakening longing. In this instance, MacDonald may also be speaking of the feminine within the man: "What I did see appeared to me perfectly lovely; more near the face that had been born with me in my soul, than anything I had seen before in nature or art."[22]

Anados tries to free the White Lady with a kiss, and eventually he begins to sing to her. As he does so, he comes to a willingness to take her deathly sleep onto himself in order to give her life, even a life with someone else: "Or if still thou choosest rather marble, be its spell on me; let thy slumber round me gather, let another dream with thee."[23] His singing indeed frees her, and she rises from the marble "a white form, veiled in a light robe

19. Ibid., 45.
20. Ibid., 76.
21. Ibid., 83.
22. Ibid.
23. Ibid., 85.

of whiteness," and then disappears into the woods, leaving Anados with an aching desire: "I gazed after her in a kind of despair; found, freed, lost! It seemed useless to follow, yet follow I must."[24]

Eventually, Anados finds the White Lady, but first he encounters numerous other feminine figures. Initially, he comes across a little maiden, "happy as a child, though she seemed almost a woman. In her hands—now in one, now in another—she carried a small globe, bright and clear as the purest crystal."[25] At first, the interaction between Anados and the little maiden is innocent. Yet as the encounter continues, it becomes clear that MacDonald is talking about sexuality, her virginity. In the previous chapter, Anados discovered his shadow, a part of himself from which he cannot be freed, a part which is self-serving, deceitful, destructive. In his desire for the globe which the maiden will not give him, he lays hold of it and will not let it go "in spite of her attempts to take it from me; yes, I shame to say, in spite of her prayers, and, at last, her tears."[26] The shadow wraps around her, and the globe bursts, releasing a black vapor. The maiden flees into the forest, "wailing like a child, and crying, 'You have broken my globe; my globe is broken—my globe is broken.'"[27] Anados, deeply regretful, loses sight of her, saying, "It lies heavy on my heart to this hour."[28] Much later—after Anados has learned to surrender his love for the White Lady—he meets this young maiden again, but as one who has learned the songs of healing and deliverance for others.

Within *Phantastes*, there is a parallel story of Cosmo, whose history, Anados says, mirrors his own. Like Anados, Cosmo encounters an unattainable, mysterious lady who begs him to set her free. Yet Cosmo hesitates, because he is "not yet pure in love."[29] The lady disappears from him, weeping that he does not love her. Eventually, Cosmo finds a way to set her free, but it costs him his life.

This story within a story leads Anados, along with the reader, another step closer to recognizing the need to encounter, love, and serve another without grasping for self-gratification. Later, while in the Fairy Queen's palace, Anados is surrounded by gracious abundance, and he begins to sing to

24. Ibid., 86.

25. Ibid., 118.

26. Ibid., 119.

27. Ibid.

28. Ibid.

29. Ibid., 166.

a statue. "And, while I sang, I did not feel that I stood by a statue, as indeed it appeared to be, but that a real woman-soul was revealing itself by successive stages of imbodiment."[30] Once again, Anados grasps for the woman: "unable to restrain myself, I sprang to her and, in defiance of the law of that place, flung my arms around her, as if I would tear her from the grasp of a visible Death."[31] But the woman eludes him, crying "You should not have touched me!"[32] and "you should have sung to me!"[33]

Anados searches for the statue-woman in deep and dark places, but he cannot find her. For as long as his love remains self-serving, it is impure and cannot be satisfied. Then, at last, Anados comes to a little cottage, where he is bidden by a sweet voice to enter. As Anados enters the cottage, he sees

> a woman-face, the most wonderful, I thought, that I had ever beheld. For it was older than any countenance I had ever looked upon. There was not a spot in which a wrinkle could lie, where a wrinkle lay not. And the skin was ancient and brown, like old parchment . . . But the moment I saw her eyes, I no longer wondered at her voice: they were absolutely young—those of a woman of five-and-twenty, large, and of a clear gray . . . the eyes were very incarnations of soft light . . . A wondrous sense of refuge and repose came upon me. I felt like a boy who has got home from school, miles across the hills, through a heavy storm of wind and snow.[34]

When Anados turns away from his selfish romantic longing towards his spiritual yearning, the Divine feminine becomes fully revealed in the face of the old wise woman. In the eternally young eyes of the old wise woman, he encounters again the eyes of the fairy woman who promised Anados a way into fairy land at the very beginning of the story. In those eyes, he finds a place of wholeness, where he sees a reflection of his most true self. This awakens a deep yearning within him, which he connects with the comfort of a mother, but also the deeper longing for God, "Him who is Father and Mother both in one."[35] Thus in the old wise woman, MacDonald links together the romantic feminine with the mother and the Divine.

---

30. Ibid., 182.
31. Ibid., 186
32. Ibid
33. Ibid., 187
34. Ibid., 202–3.
35. Ibid., 45. From his novel, *Adela Cathcart*, written a few years later.

From this cottage, Anados goes forth and finds the White Lady—while she is in the arms of her husband, a noble knight. Thus he must surrender her again and free her to the love of another. He returns to the old wise woman's cottage for comfort and guidance, and she sings healing songs to him: "Be thy heart a well of love, my child, flowing and free, and sure."[36] She helps him to relinquish the grasping love that "keeps not the spirit free" and to embrace a generous love.[37]

Along with comfort and affirmation, the wise woman gives Anados two farewell instructions. First, she encourages Anados to walk his own journey into adulthood: "Then putting her arms around me, she held me to her bosom; and as I kissed her, I felt as if I were leaving my mother for the first time, and could not help weeping bitterly. At length she gently pushed me away, and with the words, 'Go, my son, and do something worth doing,' turned back, and entering the cottage, closed the door behind her."[38] Second, after Anados repents for bringing evil upon the wise woman, she tells him not to think of that, but rather "'to do one thing. In whatever sorrow you may be, however inconsolable and irremediable it may appear, believe me that the old woman in the cottage, with the young eyes' (and she smiled), 'knows something though she must not always tell it, that would quite satisfy you about it, even in the worst moments of your distress.'"[39] The theme that all shall be well—even when evil seems to be triumphing and God does not seem to be intervening in human affairs—is revisited in a number of MacDonald's stories.

By the end, Anados is transformed. After losing his shadow, he discovers a way out of Fairy Land. Once Anados has found his way out of Fairy Land, he comforts himself with the memory of the wise woman and her wise tenderness. He finds her presence in a beech tree, which echoes his first night in Fairy Land, when he is rescued from danger by the spirit of the beech tree:

> I had lain down under the shadow of a great, ancient beech tree, that stood on the edge of the field. As I lay with my eyes closed, I began to listen to the sound of the leaves overhead. At first they made sweet inarticulate music alone; but, by-and-by, the sound seemed to begin to take shape, and to be gradually moulding itself

36. Ibid., 214.
37. Ibid.
38. Ibid., 219.
39. Ibid., 218.

into words; till, at last, I seemed able to distinguish these, half-dissolved in a little ocean of circumfluent tones: "A great good is coming—is coming—is coming to thee, Anados" and so over and over again. I fancied that the sound reminded me of the voice of the ancient woman, in the cottage that was four-square. I opened my eyes, and, for a moment, almost believed that I saw her face, with its many wrinkles and its young eyes.[40]

At the end of *Phantastes*, Anados wonders whether he can bring the lessons he learned in Fairy Land into his ordinary life. "Could I translate the experience of my travels there, into common life? This was the question."[41] He concludes, "Thus I, who set out to find my Ideal, came back rejoicing that I had lost my Shadow."[42] Drawing strength from the wise woman's words that came to him as he lay beneath the beech tree, Anados reminds himself: "Yet I know that good is coming to me—that good is always coming; though few have at all times the simplicity and the courage to believe it. What we call evil, is the only and best shape, which, for the person and his condition at the time, could be assumed by the best good."[43]

TRUSTING THE DIVINE FEMININE: *AT THE BACK OF THE NORTH WIND*

MacDonald explores the journey of coming to trust the goodness of the feminine Divine in *At the Back of the North Wind*. He wrote this story for children and for the childlike at heart when he was in his forties. The story is about a little boy named Diamond, who is the eldest son in a poor family. He sleeps in the attic, and sometimes the North Wind appears through a knothole. "Leaning over him was the large, beautiful, pale face of a woman . . . Diamond gazed at her in speechless amazement, mingled with confidence—for the boy was entranced with her mighty beauty."[44] Though sometimes a young woman and sometimes older, she is clearly a representation of the Divine.

The North Wind takes Diamond with her and speaks to him about the world and how to live well in it. He nestles in a sheltered place between her

40. Ibid., 272.
41. Ibid., 271.
42. Ibid.
43. Ibid., 273.
44. MacDonald, *At the Back of the North Wind*, 10–11

shoulder blades (at the back of the North Wind) and so only experiences the wind as gentle. Eventually, he asks to be carried so that he can feel her arms. She tells him it will not be so comfortable, but he has already learned that "there are better things than being comfortable."[45] Sometimes the North Wind brings storms, and she explains to Diamond that what seems to be destruction cannot be understood, but eventually will bring good.

The North Wind teaches Diamond about trusting in a God he cannot always understand and trusting that grace is always present, even when tragedy seems to triumph. When North Wind sinks a ship, she explains, "I often do what looks like cruel to those who do not know what I really am doing."[46] Speaking of hearing the cries from the sinking ship, she says, "'I will tell you how I am able to bear it, Diamond: I am always hearing, through every noise, through all the noise I am making myself even, the sound of a far-off song . . . Somehow, I can't say how, it tells me that all is right; that it is coming to swallow up all cries . . . It wouldn't be the song it seems to be if it did not swallow up all their fear and pain too, and set them singing it themselves with the rest."[47]

As Diamond comes to know her, he says, "I love you, and you must love me, else how did I come to love you? How could you know how to put on such a beautiful face if you did not love me and the rest. No. You may sink as many ships as you like, and I won't say another word. I can't say I shall like to see it, you know."[48]

Diamond faces a near-death experience when he lands "at the back of the North Wind," where she cannot be with him, but he learns to trust grace as the undergirding of life. In this place of transformation, he experiences the North Wind as Divine and altogether trustworthy. Through his growing maturity, he is able to care for his family when his father is ill. Thus he carries into his real world life the good that he has learned in the spiritual realm.

AWAKENING THE DIVINE FEMININE: *THE WISE WOMAN*

MacDonald further explores the interplay of God's goodness, kindness, and mystery in the *The Wise Woman*, which he wrote during his forties. As

45. Ibid., 57.
46. Ibid., 50.
47. Ibid., 47–48.
48. Ibid., 59.

noted earlier, MacDonald did not write his stories to *convey* a meaning, but to *awake* a meaning[49]—and we see this at work in *The Wise Woman*, a morality tale for parents and children, the double story of a princess and a shepherd's daughter.

In this novel, both girls are brought up believing themselves to be the center of the world. Rosamond, the princess, is vainly arrogant, and Agnes, the only child of a shepherd, is moody and selfish. The girls are each taken in by the wise woman, who kindly, but very firmly, allows them to experience the consequences of their actions in the hope that they will learn another way of being and relating with others. In the wise woman's character, MacDonald explores the character of God, whom he depicts as a female figure with magical abilities who clearly represents the loving and self-giving biblical God.

The tale of the princess recounts the long, slow journey of how the princess comes to learn responsibility. When the wise woman leaves the princess tasks to do, the princess grudgingly does them—but only when she becomes desperate for food. She decides the wise woman is fattening her up to eat her and constantly misinterprets the wise woman's firm kindness. On discovering a magical doorway in the wise woman's cottage, she cries, "'the old woman is a cheat! I believe she's an ogress after all, and lives in a palace—though she pretends it's only a cottage, to keep people from suspecting that she eats good little children like me!'"[50] She goes through the door and finds herself outside, seeing in the distance a hillside of sheep.

In the meantime, the wise woman sees that something must be done for the shepherd girl Agnes, whom MacDonald describes with wry humor: "else she would be one of those who kneel to their own shadows till feet grow on their hands till their hands grow into feet; then lay their faces on the ground till they grow into snouts; when at last they are a hideous sort of lizards, each of which believes himself the best, wisest and loveliest being in the world, yea, the very centre of the universe."[51] The wise woman takes Agnes, while Rosamond, who is following the sheep, steps into Agnes's life, learning how to live as an ordinary country girl.

Though the two girls are very different, they are similar in that "each cared more for her own fancies and desires than for anything else in the

---

49. MacDonald, "The Fantastic Imagination," in *Phantastes*, 279.

50 MacDonald, *The Wise Woman*, 75.

51. Ibid., 86–87.

world."[52] Both girls continue their separate journeys, with opportunities from the wise woman for learning and transformation. At last, the princess comes to a true understanding of herself and her need for the wise woman's help as she discovers that the wise woman is not a monster, but has been doing all for Rosamond's good. She exclaims: "How could you love such an ugly, ill-tempered, rude, hateful little wretch?"[53] The wise woman kisses her and answers: "'I saw, through it all, what you were going to be . . . But remember you have yet only begun to be what I saw.'"[54] Though Agnes is given opportunities to learn and to trust the wise woman, she continues to follow her own indulgent self-deception—all the way to the end.

The wise woman is loving and full of grace, yet she disciplines and instructs the girls through experience. She is neither punitive nor indulgent, but rather committed to their maturity and to awakening within them who they can become as they respond to who God is.

As Paul Jewett observes, "And surely most of us, especially those who are males, need to have the meaning of God our Redeemer appearing as a woman *awakened* in us. And, again, who can better help us here than a supreme master of that faculty in the human spirit by which we delight to call up new forms for old truths, the faculty which George MacDonald aptly called "the fantastic imagination"? Therefore, let all serious students of theology lay aside their Greek and Hebrew exercises, their tomes of dogmatic theology, long enough to read MacDonald's story, *The Wise Woman*, in order that they themselves may become a little wiser."[55]

CHRIST AS FEMININE DIVINE: *THE PRINCESS AND CURDIE* AND *THE PRINCESS AND THE GOBLIN*

When MacDonald was in his late forties and fifties, he wrote *The Princess and the Goblin* and *The Princess and Curdie*. Irene, the eight-year-old princess (whose mother has died) lives in a castle with her nurse and her father, the king, who is often absent. The castle is on the side of a mountain, where miners are beginning to tap into the realm of the goblins. Exploring the castle one day, Irene comes to a hidden room and discovers a beautiful and mysterious old woman who is spinning. The woman reveals that she is

52. Ibid., 94.

53. Ibid, 199.

54. Ibid.

55. Jewett, *The Ordination of Women*, 57.

Irene's great-great-grandmother and that her name is Irene as well, which means peace.

Roaming outside one day, Irene is chased by goblins, but she is rescued by Curdie, a young miner. Later, while working in the mines, Curdie discovers that the goblins plan to kidnap Irene. The great-great-grandmother gives the princess a thread which cannot be seen, but can only be felt. If followed, the thread—which is a clear metaphor for faith—will always lead her home, although it may lead her into other challenges on the way.

When the goblins finally invade the castle, a mysterious woman-turned-scullery maid (whom we later learn is the great-great grandmother in disguise) secures their defeat. Her identity is revealed when she shares a meal and pours a cup of red wine. In these books, the woman is a clear Christ figure, "the source of light and is called 'the Mother of Light,' which correlates with MacDonald's name for God, which is the 'Father of Lights.'"[56] Kerry Dearborn describes the great-great-grandmother as "a great queen, but humbles herself to become a servant maid who is beaten yet brings about the defeat of evil; she is both judge and the one who is judged; she is described as the 'one centre of harmony and loveliness' in whom 'the whole creation seemed gathered.'"[57] Throughout these novels, MacDonald seeks to awaken in readers their need of God and their own need for further transformation in the journey of faith.

DARKNESS AND SELF-DECEPTION, SELF-KNOWLEDGE AND LIGHT: *LILITH*

MacDonald wrote *Phantastes* in his thirties and *Lilith* forty years later. In both stories, a man sets out on a journey of self-discovery, a spiritual journey towards a deepening knowledge of God. The tone of *Lilith* is markedly different from *Phantastes*, for in *Lilith* there is a dark presence, a sense of evil. This presence deceives Vane, the main character. In mythical terms, Lilith was Adam's first wife, who turned to evil, much as Lucifer does in the Bible. Early in the story, Vane meets Eve, Adam's second wife: "her face luminous, but the eyes . . . large, and dark with a darkness ever deepening as I gazed. A whole night-heaven lay condensed in each pupil . . . her eyes must have been coming direct out of [God's] own!"[58] Eve represents a loving

---

56. Dearborn, *Baptized Imagination*, 69, n. 11.

57. Ibid.

58. MacDonald, *Lilith*, 27.

female as an immortal deity,[59] "the mother of us all, the lady of the New Jerusalem."[60]

Adam and Eve watch over those who sleep. Sleep is a metaphor for death, but also an invitation to surrender to God's transformative work. Vane resists this surrender and so is challenged to rescue the Little Ones, a group of children who need to be guided to safety. In this journey, Vane is aided by Lona, who is an archetype of the virginal lover. Through the journey, Vane is tempted and deceived by Lilith, a destructive yet romantic figure, who is deeply attractive to Vane's ego. Like *Phantastes*, *Lilith* is a story of the human journey, where we must confront our own ego and vanity in order to come to painful self-knowledge and surrender to God.

In a brief biography and commentary, Nick Page identifies *Lilith* as MacDonald's masterpiece. He describes it as "a dense, haunting book," reworked four times, "digging deeper into the mystery and meaning of the spiritual journey [MacDonald] had been travelling."[61] MacDonald's biographer William Raeper recognizes how *Lilith* reflects MacDonald's own journey: "In many ways *Lilith* was the book MacDonald had been trying to write all his life, indeed had been writing all his life, and even after he had finished it he was excruciatingly aware of its shortcomings and inadequacies."[62] Yet there is much beauty and hope within its pages—and there is even hope for Lilith's eventual redemption.

Throughout his life, MacDonald explored this journey of deeper self-knowledge, always aware of the presence of self-deception. His early loss of his mother likely sparked his awareness of his deep masculine need for the feminine within the Divine. His use of fantasy and poetry released him from the constraints of propositional language and analytical conceptualization, freeing him to identify women as guides and representatives of God's grace and kindness. In his journey and in the journey of his characters, the spiritual life and surrender to God offered a salvation from lust and self-centeredness, and the feminine presence of God became a counterbalance to the dark forces of egoism and rationalism.

59. Mendelson, "George MacDonald's *Lilith*," 208.

60. Ibid., 147

61. Page, "Introduction" in *Phantastes*, 29.

62. Raeper, *George MacDonald*, 365.

7

Holy Wisdom as Friend and Lover

Thomas Merton

God is not only a Father but a Mother. He is both at the same time, and it is the "feminine aspect" or "feminine principle" in the divinity that is the Hagia Sophia [Holy Wisdom].[1]

LIFE JOURNEY

The life of Thomas Merton (1915–1968) was marked by paradox. He was both a hermit and a social activist. He lived as a celibate monk and yet fell in love with a woman. He wrestled honestly with both great ideas and human relationships, relating deeply with many people around the world while living as "the first Cistercian hermit since the Middle Ages."[2]

Merton was born in France to a New Zealander father and an American mother who were both artists. While he was a baby, his family moved

---

1. Merton, *A Life in Letters*, 183.
2. Griffin, *Follow the Ecstasy*, xii

to live near his grandparents in New York, where his younger brother was born. As a child, he was not close to his mother, who died of cancer when he was six years old. In his autobiography, Merton remembers his mother: "I have seen a picture of her as a rather slight, thin, sober little person with a serious and somewhat anxious and very sensitive face. And this corresponds with my memory of her—worried, precise, quick, critical of me, her son."[3]

But when he was five, he experienced the brief love of a mother figure during a visit from his father's mother. He remembers: "I was most of all impressed by Granny. She must have talked to me a great deal, and asked me many questions and told me a great number of things, and though there are few precise details I remember about that visit, the general impression she left was one of veneration and awe—and love."[4] She taught him the "Our Father" and "after that I did not forget it."[5]

When his mother was hospitalized, he did not understand much of what was happening. Of that time, he writes: "Everything about sickness and death was more or less kept hidden from me, because consideration of these things might make a child morbid . . . I was never even taken to the hospital to see Mother, after she went there. And this was entirely her own idea."[6] Recalling his early experience of being separated from his mother, he reflects:

> I did not miss Mother very much, and did not weep when I was not allowed to go and see her. Then one day Father gave me a note to read. I was very surprised. It was for me personally and it was in my mother's handwriting. I don't think she had ever written to me before—there had never been any occasion for it. Then I understood what was happening, although, as I remember, the language of the letter was confusing to me. Nevertheless, one thing was quite evident. My mother was informing me, by mail, that she was about to die, and would never see me again.[7]

Thirty years later, Merton wrote in his journal: "In the natural order, perhaps solitaries are made by severe mothers."[8] Adding to this experience

3. Merton, *Seven Storey Mountain*, 5.
4. Ibid., 9.
5. Ibid., 9.
6. Ibid., 14.
7. Ibid., 14.
8. Merton, *The Intimate Merton*, 76.

of "severe mothers," Merton's father began an affair with another woman, Evelyn, who was very hard on Thomas. Evelyn's son said later: "my mother was ruthlessly and uncouthly indifferent to whatever his private sorrows and obsessions might have been."[9] Merton's father broke off the affair and moved to France, where Thomas spent two years in a French Catholic boarding school while his brother stayed in New York with his grandparents. Then Thomas and his father moved to England, where Thomas boarded at an English Protestant school. For the next two years, as Merton puts it, "I think I was almost sincerely religious."[10]

Then when Merton was fifteen, his father died, and his "religious phase"[11] ended, for Merton lost his interest in faith for the rest of his school years. But when Merton left school and travelled to Rome, something drew him to the Catholic churches, and he began to read the New Testament. One night, he experienced his father's presence in the room with him, and he recognized the emptiness of his life. He commented in his biography that after this, for the first time, he really prayed.[12]

Merton returned to England to attend the University of Cambridge and soon seemed to lose the longing for God he had experienced in Rome. As his life became more and more dissolute, he fathered a child. His shame over this ran deep, and guilt over his behavior clouded his life. "He had longed for love but had found instead how easy it is to father an unwanted child. He had no further contact with the girl or her child, and because of this was deeply troubled by guilt."[13] This seems to have been the last straw for his guardian, who sent him back in disgrace to live with his grandparents in New York.[14] A few years later, in an application for a role with Friendship House in Harlem, he wrote, "once I did get in some trouble, enough for it to be an impediment to my becoming a *priest* . . . it is something that definitely demands a whole life of penance."

Once back in New York, he began to study literature at Columbia University. A year later, his grandfather died. Merton recounts that without thinking about it, he knelt and prayed. He began to read about Catholicism, and gradually God became more meaningful to him. Over the next

9. Shaw, *Beneath the Mask of Holiness*, 149.

10. Merton, *The Seven Storey Mountain*, 65.

11. Ibid., 65.

12. Merton, *The Seven Storey Mountain*, 111.

13. Furlong, *Merton*, 61.

14. Elie, *The Life You Save May Be Your Own*, 41–42.

few years, he continued to study, completing his bachelor's and master's degrees, while also questioning the possibility of becoming a monk.

When he was twenty-six, after exploring several possibilities, he joined the Cistercians at the Abbey of Gethsemani, Kentucky. His superior recognized his writing gift and encouraged him to write. When he was thirty-three, his biography *The Seven Storey Mountain*[15] was published to great public acclaim. For the next twenty years, Merton wrote and served as a novice master at Gethsemani, nurturing solitude as a way of life while also engaging in correspondence and activism. In the later years, in spite of his hiddenness and silence, he began to travel extensively and have enormous influence on the "outside" world.

ENCOUNTERING HOLY WISDOM: *HAGIA SOPHIA*

Throughout the 1950s and 1960s, Merton's books, journal reflections, and correspondence reveal the development of his spirituality and the evolution of his changing theology. In particular, Merton recognizes the importance of the work that needed to happen within him. "If I can unite in *myself*, in my own spiritual life, the thought of the East and the West of the Greek and Latin Fathers, I will create in myself a reunion of the divided church and from that unity in myself can come the exterior and visible unity of the church. For if we want to bring together East and West we cannot do it by imposing one upon the other. We must contain both in ourselves and transcend both in Christ."[16]

One of the important shifts that happened within him was the evolution of his understanding of Sophia (Wisdom) as God. In 1957, Merton encountered Hagia Sophia "while reading Russian mystics, who were fascinated with those passages in the Book of Proverbs in which 'Wisdom is "playing in the world" before the face of the Creator.'"[17] From this time on, Christ as Wisdom of God—as Sophia—became large in Merton's religious imagination. "One has only to read the journals from 1957 through 1961 to be struck by the frequency and poignancy with which the Wisdom figure of the Hebrew Scriptures began to haunt Merton's religious imagination, thanks largely to his close study of Russian Orthodox sophiology."[18] During

15. First published as *Elected Silence* in the United Kingdom.

16. Merton, *A Search for Solitude*, 87.

17. Forest, *Living with Wisdom*, 131.

18. Ibid., 153.

this time period, Merton also began to exchange letters with the Orthodox priest Boris Pasternak, who eventually became one of his "wisdom" mentors.[19]

Then in February 1958, Merton dreamt that a young Jewish girl embraced him and told him her name was Proverb. The dream impacted him so deeply that he wrote her several letters, thanking her for loving him and "awakening in him things he thought he had lost forever."[20] He also wrote about the dream to Boris Pasternak: "One night I dreamt that I was sitting with a very young Jewish girl of fourteen or fifteen, and that she suddenly manifested a very deep and pure affection for me and embraced me so that I was moved to the depths of my soul. I learned that her name was 'Proverb,' which I thought very simple and beautiful . . . Thus you are initiated into the scandalous secret of a monk who is in love with a girl, and a Jew at that!"[21]

Eighteen months later, while in hospital for X-rays, he was gently awakened from a dream by a nurse. He recounts: "it was like awakening for the first time from all the dreams of my life—as if the Blessed Virgin herself, as if Wisdom had awakened me. We do not hear her soft voice, the gentle voice, the feminine voice, the voice of the Mother: yet she speaks everywhere and in everything. Wisdom cries out in the marketplace—'if anyone is little let him come to me.'"[22] In this dream encounter, Merton is being drawn toward the feminine Divine. In Jungian understanding, we might say that Merton was engaging with the anima, seeking to discover and integrate the feminine within himself and as a dimension of God.

As Merton continued to explore Hagia Sophia, he visited his friend, the artist Victor Hammer, at his home in 1959, where he saw a painting of Christ as a boy being crowned by a woman who is standing behind him. Merton asked about the identity of the woman, and Hammer answered that he had begun by painting a Madonna and child, but the picture had turned out differently, and he didn't know who the woman was. Merton answered, "I know who she is. I have always known her. She is Hagia Sophia."[23]

After Merton's visit, Hammer wrote and asked him to say more about Hagia Sophia. Merton's response reflects his struggle to name such ideas:

19. Pramuk, *Sophia*, 129.

20. Waldron, *The Wounded Heart of Thomas Merton*, 72.

21. Merton, *A Life in Letters*, 108.

22. Ibid., 13.

23. Merton, *A Life in Letters*, 183.

. . . it is most difficult to write anything that really makes sense about this most mysterious reality in the mystery of God—Hagia Sophia (Holy Wisdom).The first thing to be said, of course, is that Hagia Sophia is God Himself. God is not only a Father but a Mother. He is both at the same time, and it is the "feminine aspect" or "feminine principle" in the divinity that is the Hagia Sophia. But of course as soon as you say this the whole thing becomes misleading: a division of an "abstract" divinity into two abstract principles. Nevertheless, to ignore this distinction is to lose touch with the fullness of God.[24]

In trying to articulate Hagia Sophia further, Merton calls her "the dark nameless *Ousia* [Being]" of God."[25] After this time, he begins to see the feminine as "not one of the Three Divine Persons, but each 'at the same time, are Sophia and manifest her.'"[26]

Christopher Pramuk comments on Merton's slow inner journey in coming to such a knowing of Sophia: "It involves the slow and sensitive discernment of who God is, and who we are, through long meditation on the images and poetical symbols that shine through quietly, like forgotten stars, or break through dangerously, like flashes of lightning, from the revelatory firmament of the Bible."[27] As the poet, Susan McCaslin writes, "The efforts to name Sophia, to catch her in the net of language defer to the apophatic tradition of 'unnaming'. Every naming becomes an unnaming, a backing off from language, and an insistence that words are inadequate before mystery. Sophia herself becomes 'the unknown, the dark, the nameless,'" reminding us that "God is not an object of knowledge. The God who is male and female, father and mother, is simultaneously neither male nor female, transcending gender categories."[28]

After four years of this slow and sensitive discernment period, Merton wrote "Hagia Sophia," a prose poem of two thousand words, which was published in 1963. The poem reflects the impossibility of netting God in language, except perhaps as a poet seeing through a glass darkly, for "Sophia is Gift, is Spirit, *Donum Dei*. She is God-given and God Himself as Gift."[29]

24   Ibid., 183 (Letter to the artist Victor Hammer, 14 May 1959).

25.   Pramuk, *Sophia*, 194.

26.   Ibid., 194.

27.   Ibid., 209.

28.   McCaslin, "Merton and Hagia Sophia," 248–249.

29.   Merton, "Hagia Sophia," 69

The poem is divided into sections named by the quarters of the monastic day. It begins with the image of a vulnerable man who is lying in a hospital bed, being cared for by the feminine. Early in the morning, he is awakened from a dream by a soft voice:

> Such is the awakening of one man, one morning, at
> the voice of a nurse in the hospital. Awakening out
> of languor and darkness, out of helplessness, out of
> sleep, newly confronting reality and finding it to be
> gentleness.[30]

The second section, "Early Morning," names Sophia as Wisdom, feminine, and childlike: "one Wisdom, one Child, one Meaning, one Sister." In the third and longest section, "High Morning," Merton explores God as both feminine and masculine:

> All the perfections of created things are also in God;
> and therefore He is at once Father and Mother. As
> Father He stands in solitary might surrounded by
> darkness. As Mother His shining is diffused, embracing
> all His creatures with merciful tenderness and light.
> The Diffuse Shining of God is Hagia Sophia.
> We call her His "glory." In Sophia His power is
> experienced only as mercy and as love.[31]

The final section, "Compline," depicts the "crowning of the Divine son with his human nature" by the humble Sophia:

> She crowns Him not with what is glorious, but with
> what is greater than glory: the one thing greater than
> glory is weakness, nothingness, poverty[32].

Pramuk observes that this poem invites us to consider:

> What would be the effect on the Christian (and human) community of remembering God not only as a "Person" (Jesus Christ) but as a Woman, calling out tenderly from the crossroads, urging the peoples of the world to come together and to recognize one another as members of one diverse, but radically interdependent, family? As a Mother, bent over her children in fierce protection, or

---

30. Ibid., 66.
31. Ibid., 68.
32. Ibid.

crowning them with purpose and strength for the difficult journey ahead?[33]

He further notes the significance of Merton using "gendered metaphors interchangeably in "Hagia Sophia" 'to suggest a presence and power beyond' traditional gender binaries.'"[34] Yet he also cautions that "we should not be too quick to move 'beyond' female images (and names) of God prior to having lingered with them for a very long while, allowing depths of memory, thought, and feeling to rise to the surface . . . The poem disrupts all self-enclosed worldviews, every arrogance, idolatry, patriarchy, or religious fundamentalism that would justify the erasure or diminishment of persons, any person, in the name of God."[35] Pramuk is thus inviting us to the inner work of integrating the masculine and feminine. Similarly, poet Susan McCaslin notes the fluidity of Merton's metaphors, where Sophia "is not just the feminine face of a masculine God, or a masculine God with feminine attributes (God in a skirt), but an active power permeating all things."[36]

Merton's understanding of the feminine presence within the Divine emphasizes the humility of God. Merton draws from the description of Wisdom in Proverbs 8: "Then I was beside him, as a master workman; and I was daily his delight, rejoicing always before him. Rejoicing in the world, his earth, and having my delight in the sons of men" (8:30–31, NASB). In Merton's response to Victor Hammer, he describes Sophia as "the center and meaning of all, that which is the smallest and poorest and most humble of all: the 'feminine child,' playing before God the Creator in His universe, 'playing before Him at all times, playing in the world' (Proverbs 8)."[37] The interpretation of playfulness is found in the Douay-Rheims Bible: "I was with him forming all things: and was delighted every day, playing before him at all times."[38] Merton reflects on this innocence, humility, and playfulness: "Sophia, the feminine child, is playing in the world. Obvious and unseen, playing at all times before the Creator."[39] He also emphasizes the poverty and humility of God: "That which is poorest and humblest, that

33. Pramuk, *Sophia*, 208.

34. Ibid., 209.

35. Ibid., 210.

36. McCaslin, "Merton and Hagia Sophia," 253.

37. Merton, *A Life in Letters*, 183.

38. Proverbs 8:30, Douay-Rheims.

39. Merton, "Hagia Sophia," 69.

which is most hidden." Then, a few lines later, the naming of God is reduced to Nothing ("*Exinanivit semetipsum*"), which echoes the self-emptying of Philippians 2:7.

Perhaps the most profound discovery of "Hagia Sophia" is the revelation that God is most God in this humblest of places, the feminine child, the one who crowns Christ, sending him into the world in human form, in humility, nakedness, and brokenness. As another line in the poem expresses it, "She is the Bride and the Feast and the Wedding." Pramuk notes the challenge of expressing this integration of opposites. Merton "carries us beyond the dialectic of positive/negative theology into a kind of mystical third moment, where idols are shattered—not in the silence of negation, but in the plenitude of affirmation—and where there is unity in difference and ecstatic praise. In short, Merton ushers us into a mosaic experience of God brimming with positive content, spilling over its linguistic containers."[40]

Merton's "Hagia Sophia" reflects an intense engagement with God—the God of poverty and nothingness, the God who is open to humiliation and vulnerability. By opening himself to the Spirit, being willing to make mistakes in order to learn, and wrestling with this humble God, Merton reckons with the deep longings of his heart and embarks on a profound journey of transformation. Reflecting on this journey, he writes: "It is a profound event in my life and one which will have entered deeply into my heart to alter and transform my whole climate of thought and experience."[41]

Thus "By the early 1960s, Thomas Merton had embraced the sophiological worldview fully as his own, and had begun to translate it with intellectual and poetic vitality to the West."[42] Robert Waldron, a Jungian commentator on Thomas Merton's life and spiritual journey, notes that the "Hagia Sophia" poem "charts Merton's journey from his previous 'refusal of women' to his acceptance of the feminine principle in his life."[43]

A few years later, Merton's love affair with a young nurse grounded his search for the feminine Divine in real life.

40. Pramuk, *Sophia*, 204.
41. Merton, "Mid Summer Diary," 328, 328 (22 June 1966).
42. Ibid., 177.
43. Waldron, *Wounded Heart*, 75.

ENCOUNTERING THE FEMININE IN LIFE AND LOVE

Many writers have commented on Merton's difficult relationships with women—the loss of his mother as a child, his father's affair with Evelyn, his lack of parenting through his teenage years, his womanizing during his Cambridge years, his vows as a monk in his mid-twenties, and then his romantic devotion to Mary. "For Merton, the issue of loving a woman and attaining better understanding of his relationship with his mother are frequently repeated throughout his writings."[44]

Kenneth Bragan, who explores the theme of the feminine in Merton's life from a Jungian perspective, explains: "at the 'core,' the intense early experience he'd had with his mother . . . was buried deep within."[45] As Merton engaged with the feminine, first by naming Compassion as his Lady in 1951,[46] "there was sufficient 'maternal' presence at the 'core' for him to start to be able to live fully and passionately."[47] He had to complete this "inward journey of getting to the fullness of his self . . . Going to the 'core' had still been going to the place of his mother's absence."[48] During these years, the "feminine presence" was strengthened within Merton as he responded to the feminine in God, engaged with the *anima* in dreams and through his active imagination, and as he began to relate to women. Bragan identifies Merton's friendship with Naomi Burton, who "was a 'real presence' to support the archetypal presences in his inner world."[49] In a journal entry from 1965, Merton reflects on the importance of Burton's "realistic understanding and feminine comfort" as he identifies his *"refusal* of woman which is a fault in my chastity."[50]

Then in the journals that Merton kept between 1966 and 1967, he traces an honest account of his love affair with Margie Smith, a young student nurse, whom he met while in the hospital for an operation on his back. His account of his initial encounter of Margie is very similar to the experience he describes in "Hagia Sophia," which he had written four years earlier.

44. Kramp, "Merton's Melancholia," 441–58.

45. Bragan, *The Making of a Saint*, 7.

46. Merton, *The Sign of Jonas*, 323–24.

47. Ibid., 79.

48. Ibid., 85.

49. Ibid., 100.

50. Merton, *Dancing in the Water of Life*, 281 (17 August 1965). Italics in the original.

In recalling his time in the hospital, Merton recognizes the luxury of being cared for so intimately by a woman. He says, "I realized that though I am pretty indifferent to the society of my fellow monks (can live without being lonely for the community *at all*, and it is a work of will to go down and participate in the essentials, not an emotional need), I do feel a deep emotional need for feminine companionship and love, and seeing that I must irrevocably live without it ended up by tearing me up more than the operation itself."[51] In the same entry, he mentions the student nurse who particularly cares for him and converses with him.

We come to know that student nurse as M, (as he calls her in his diaries), whose caring responsiveness for Merton leads him to prolong his contact with her. During this time, he makes the surprising discovery that his deepest sense of being who God made him to be is revealed in his relationship with Margie rather than in his life as a hermit. He reflects: "I think, if the truth be told, what I am looking for is not to 'be a hermit' but just to be myself, the person God made me to be—and also incidentally the person loved by M."[52]

Throughout his time in hospital, and on later visits for further appointments, he and Margie continue to spend time together. And after returning to the monastery, he begins to call Margie on the phone—something he should have asked permission to do, but does not. His diary entries throughout these months trace the pendulum swings of his overwhelming sense of love for her and his self-recrimination, since what he is doing brings his whole way of life into question.

"She has settled down to a sweet little-girl happiness that completely disarms and ravishes me. I just don't know what to do with my life, finding myself so much loved and loving so much, when according to all standards it is all wrong, absurd, insane."[53] The following day, he writes: ". . . and the meaning of everything that ever happened was suddenly centered in us because we were now love. It was our turn to express and show forth in worship the essence of all truth and life and meaning by our love."[54] A few days later, he reflects on how the experience of falling in love has opened up wells within him that he has never known before. "I have never seen so much simple, spontaneous, total love. And I realize that the deepest capaci-

51. Merton, *Learning to Love*, 38 (10 April 1966).
52. Ibid., 48 (28 April 1996).
53. Ibid., 50 (4 May 1966).
54. Ibid., 50.

ties for human love in me have never even been tapped, that I too can love with an awful completeness. Responding to her has opened up the depths of my life in ways I can't begin to understand and analyze now."[55]

He tries desperately to find ways to keep his intense love for Margie—and hers for him—without breaking his vows, though he knows very early on that this is fruitless. Yet he is also conscious that he is receiving deep healing as he allows himself to love and be loved. A month after his stay in hospital he writes:

> I have surrendered again to a kind of inimical womanly wisdom in M. which instinctively seeks out the wound in me that most needs her sweetness, and lavishes all her love upon me there . . . I feel that somehow my sexuality has made me real and decent again after years of rather frantic suppression (for though I thought I had it all truly controlled, this was an illusion). I feel less sick, I feel human, I am grateful for her love which is so totally mine. All the beauty of it comes from this that we are not just playing; we belong totally to each other's love (except for the vow that prevents the last complete surrender).[56]

This vow continually calls Merton back from consummating the relationship. And when one of his illicit phone conversations is overheard, he confesses to his superior, who kindly but firmly tells him he must cease contact with Margie.

Nevertheless, that June, he writes a "Mid Summer Diary" for her, where he reflects on what the opening of love has meant for him and his relationship with God. For through the passion he feels for Margie and the earthiness of ordinary life, he is drawn into deeper self-knowing and knowing of God. He speaks of "plunging through the center of his own nothingness and coming out into the All which is the Void and which is . . . the Love of God."[57] And a day or two later: "I cannot regard this as 'just an episode.' It is a profound event in my life and one which will have entered deeply into my heart to alter and transform my whole climate of thought and experience: for in her love I now realize I had found something, someone, that I

---

55. Ibid., 50.

56. Ibid., 66–67 (20 May 1966).

57. Merton, "Mid Summer Diary," 324 (20 June 1966).

had been looking for all my life."[58] As Kenneth Bragan notes, "his love affair had opened his heart. He revelled in it."[59]

Yet because Merton and Margie encountered one another at such different places in the life journey, they "experienced the wrenching tension of their radically different life-styles and commitments—the monk in his early fifties, the student nurse in her early twenties; the vowed celibate and the young woman ready for marriage; the solitary and the college co-ed; the spiritual master and the professional novice. These staggering differences in history and temperament cast their love into the shadows of profound ambiguity and anxiety."[60]

This roller-coaster continues for some months, with Merton finding ways to contact Margie and then regretting his actions, all the while reflecting on what this opening of love means, and how he understands it in relation to God. As Suzanne Zuercher observes: "He has periods of wisdom when he realizes that at fifty-one there is an embarrassing adolescence in what's happening to him. (It seems to be happening to Margie as well, although it is more appropriate to her in her twenties.) Despite his infatuation, Merton's years as a monk committed to spiritual reflection at the most profound level have taught him the ability to critique the situation."[61]

When Merton finally ends the relationship at the end of that summer and renews his vows, he remains deeply aware of the healing that has come through their relationship. "There is a certain fullness in my life now, even without her. Something that was never there before."[62] Two days later, he writes: "Was I being faithful in an obscure way to some other and more inscrutable call that was from God? Somehow I can't help believing that I was. The conviction will not leave me."[63]

Thus by interacting with the concrete reality of a particular woman, Merton encounters the Divine feminine in a profoundly new way, which deepens his love for God—and, eventually, his commitment to a life of solitude. A brief but significant diary entry reveals how his journey with Margie has drawn him towards the feminine Divine: "Strange connection in my deepest heart—between M. and the "Wisdom" figure—and Mary—and

58. Ibid., 328 (22 June 1966).

59. Bragan, *The Making of a Saint*, 123.

60. Cozzens, *The Changing Face of the Priesthood*, 41–42

61. Zuercher, *The Ground of Love and Truth*, 52–53.

62. Merton, *Learning to Love*, 119 (2 September 1966).

63. Ibid., 121 (4 September 1966).

the Feminine in the Bible—Eve etc.—Paradise—wisdom. (Most mysterious, haunting, deep, lovely, moving, transforming!)"[64] Two months later, he reflects: "Somehow in the depths of my being I know that love for her can co-exist with my solitude."[65] And the following winter, he writes: "still retaining a warm and deep affection for her . . . my love has been far too deep to be abandoned."[66]

Yet a year after meeting Margie, Merton continues to struggle with his choices and what the encounter has meant:

> I experience in myself a deep need of conversion and penance—
> a deep repentance, a real sense of having erred, gone wrong, got
> lost—and needing to get back on the right path. Needing to pray
> for forgiveness. Sense of revolt at my own foolishness and triviality. Shame and amazement at the way I have trifled with life and
> grace—how could I be so utterly stupid! A real sense of being
> flawed and of needing immense help, pardon—to recover some
> capacity to love God. Sense of the nearness and mercy of Mary.[67]

Though he has moved away from a relationship with the 'outer feminine,' he acknowledges his deep inner need for the feminine Divine—"the mercy of Mary."

Merton's biographer Monica Furlong observes that his relationship with Margie "may have been very important for Merton's full recognition of his own wholeness, his creative blend of male and femaleness."[68] Similarly, in an interview with Morgan Atkinson (who made a documentary about Merton), Paul Pearson notes: "After his relationship with [Margie] in 1966 he no longer talks about that difficulty [his lack of a mother figure], so I think it enabled him to make some kind of breakthrough."[69] Robert Waldron makes a similar connection: "For him truly to solve his 'refusal of woman,' he had to fall in love with a woman and it is actually what happened. In 'Hagia Sophia,' he offers this description of himself (and the God within him): 'A vagrant, a destitute wanderer. . .'"[70] Merton's "destitute" wandering eventually weaves together the feminine within himself and God.

64. Merton, *Learning to Love*, 131 (10 September 1966).

65. Ibid., 162 (16 November 1966).

66. Ibid., 193 (6 February 1967).

67. Ibid., 234 (13 May 1967).

68. Furlong, *Merton*, 314.

69. Atkinson, *Soul Searching*, 165.

70. Waldron, *The Wounded Heart of Thomas Merton*, 155.

Perhaps the final lines of his "Hagia Sophia" best express where he eventually found himself after his tumultuous love affair with Margie, for he fully identifies with Christ: "She [Sophia] sends the infinitely Rich and Powerful One forth as poor and helpless, in His mission of inexpressible mercy, to die for us on the Cross . . . A homeless God . . . lies down in desolation under the sweet stars of the world and entrusts himself to sleep."[71]

Eighteen months later, on the tenth of December 1968, while attending an interfaith conference in Thailand, Thomas Merton died from accidental electrocution (presumably from a faulty electrical fan in his room). He had just given a lecture, which he completed with a plea for openness to the "painfulness of inner change" and the statement, "What is essential . . . is concerned with this business of total inner transformation."[72] As Furlong notes, these words and even the manner of his death were a reflection of who he was: "It had an element of surprise, of drama, of unusualness, and even, despite the overwhelming sadness of his friends and brothers, a kind of black humor about it that fitted both the boy Merton had been, and the man he had become."

CONCLUSION

Thomas Merton's life traces an unfolding journey of masculine-feminine integration. Merton identifies the long-term impact of his lack of feminine love in childhood and his mother's severity, and he also recognizes the problematic nature of his sexual relationships with women during his university years, which were followed by a "refusal of women" when he entered a celibate life. In the adoration of Mary, he found a way to respond to and receive feminine love.

Throughout his journals, Merton's honesty and stringent self-examination led him to become more open to the human feminine and the feminine in God. A parallel journey of openness to female friendship and to Hagia Sophia, which culminated in his love affair with Margie, healed a deep wound in Merton and enabled him to accept himself as a sexual man, able to love and be loved.

71. Merton, "Hagia Sophia," 71.
72. Furlong, Merton, 330.

8

"My, my, my, how I do love you!"
Paul Young

"Mack, look at you!" she [Papa God] fairly exploded. "Here you are, and so grown up. I have really been looking forward to seeing you face-to-face. It is so wonderful to have you here with us. My, my, my, how I do love you!"[1]

William Paul Young was born in 1955 in Grand Prairie, Alberta, Canada as the eldest of four children. He grew up as a missionary child in Netherlands New Guinea (West Papua) among the Dani, a technologically stone age tribal people. He now lives in the United States with his wife, Kim. Together, they have six children and (at the time of writing) twelve grandchildren. Paul[2] has had a varied career both in business and church contexts, often writing as a creative expression.

In 2005 he wrote *The Shack* for his children and, at the encouragement of friends, published it two years later. The novel tells the story of Mackenzie ("Mack"), who is drawn into relationship with the God of love after his daughter, Missy, is sexually molested and murdered. Within thirteen months, *The Shack* sold its first million copies and in eight years, twenty million. In 2012, Paul published *Cross Roads*, a novel about an egotistical

1. Young, *The Shack*, 77.

2. In this chapter, I refer to Paul by his first name, since some of this material came from personal interviews and email correspondence.

businessman who, as he faces death, meets God in the authenticity of others and his own unexpected inner journey. Paul believes that his books have become popular because they resonate with the "tuning fork" people have within them—the great sadness, the longing for the God of profound grace, the God who is not a masculine hierarchy, but a dance of mutual love.

EARLY JOURNEY

In describing his childhood, Paul writes: "I thought the way I grew up was 'normal' but most would probably agree that my history and journey have been a bit unusual."[3] He describes how the Dani people "became my family and as the first white child and outsider who ever spoke their language, I was granted unusual access into their culture and community." He explains that the Dani were "at times a fierce warring people, steeped in the worship of spirits and even occasionally practicing ritualistic cannibalism," yet "they also provided a deep sense of identity that remains an indelible element of my character and person." By the time he attended boarding school at age six (as was the policy of his denomination), he says: "I was in most respects a white Dani."[4] These are the facts of Paul's childhood, but his novels trace an inner journey, and name "The Great Sadness" which Paul has lived with from his childhood and through much of his adult life.

This great sadness was formed by three major factors in Paul's life. First, Paul had a very problematic relationship with his father, who as a pastor and missionary was able to care for others, but had unrealistic expectations of his oldest son, and he responded to Paul's failure to meet his expectations with anger. Paul says his childhood memories of his father are brutal, and he has no memories of his mother, whom he describes as a "follower." His parents were so involved in their missionary work that when he first came back from boarding school, he called his mom Aunt Betty because that was the name of the white woman at the school.

The second factor that contributed to Paul's great sadness was his experience of sexual abuse. As a young child, he was sexually abused by Dani men in his father's mission. And then when he was sent away to boarding school at age six, he was sexually abused by the older boys. Of the sexual abuse in *The Shack*, Paul writes: "The pain in the story is very real. My shack

3. These quotes are from Paul's website http://wmpaulyoung.com/wm-paul-young-about/

4. Young, "Wm. Paul Young," lines 8–18.

has a lot to do with the fact that sexual abuse started very young within the culture that I was a part of, and then unfortunately, at the mission boarding school."[5]

The third major factor that formed Paul's great sadness was his experience of culture shock and dislocation when, as Paul writes: "In the middle of a school year, my family unexpectedly returned to the West. My father worked as a Pastor for a number of small churches in Western Canada and by the time I graduated, I had already attended thirteen different schools."[6] His reflection on these experiences gives the sense of the impact they had on him: ". . . the disconnect and the culture shock and then being yanked out of there and put back into the western world, which I didn't understand at all, without healing any of this damage that was beneath the surface. . ."[7]

JOURNEY INTO ADULTHOOD

Paul paid his way through Warner Pacific College in Portland, Oregon by working as a radio disc jockey, lifeguard, and in the oil fields of northern Alberta. After graduating with a degree in religion, he married Kim Warren and began working at a large suburban church while attending seminary. To support their growing family, he worked in various fields—insurance, construction, telecommunications, contract work, food processing, business start-ups.[8]

Yet by keeping his childhood wounding hidden, he was living a false persona. Of this experience, Paul writes; "then you just become a performer and at the same time, you hold all of these pieces of your heart that have been broken, you hold them together by any way you can and a lot of it is by lying, by presenting one thing but knowing that there is a mess underneath the whole thing."[9] Somehow, Paul continued to perform to the world's demands, though his desperate struggle for wholeness was becoming unbearable. Of the disconnect between his external and internal life, he observes that the "facts don't tell you about the pain of trying to adjust to different cultures, of life losses that were almost too staggering to bear, of walking down railroad tracks at night in the middle of winter screaming

5. Robinson, "James Robinson and The Shack," lines 61–63.
6. Young, "Wm. Paul Young," lines 19–22.
7. Robinson, "James Robinson and The Shack," lines 91–93.
8. Young, "Wm. Paul Young," lines 22–32.
9. Robinson, "James Robinson and The Shack," lines 94–97.

into the windstorm, of living with an underlying volume of shame so deep and loud that it constantly threatened any sense of sanity, of dreams not only destroyed but obliterated by personal failure, of hope so tenuous that only the trigger seemed to offer a solution."[10]

By the time he was thirty-eight, the depth of the wounding was taking its toll. Of this time, he writes: "So here I am and trying to hold this all together and that kind of damage breaks you into pieces. You're constantly trying to present the best but there is failure underneath."[11] He adds that "when men realize they can't compete anymore . . . they will look to some imagination of relationship—hoping someone tells them they have worth. So their vulnerability then is to an affair."[12] During this time, Paul had a three-month affair, which he says was no more authentic than his relationship with his wife. But he imagined that he and this other woman had a great destiny. His fantasies were filled with delusions of grandeur. Paul explains that the facade and his delusions were not consciously duplicitous, but he was trying to protect his pain and shame with addictions and failures so that others would not see his real person and hate him as much as he hated himself. Paul's struggle reflects the shared experience of many others who have been sexually abused, for "the trauma of sexual abuse leads to deep shame, and frequently unhealthy sexual expression in adulthood."[13]

A single phone call rocked his world forever—two words, in fact: "I know." When his wife, Kim, found out about the affair he was having with one of her friends, he determined to tell her all his secrets in order to save their marriage. It took four ten-hour days to tell her absolutely everything. The shack became a metaphor for the place where he had previously hidden all his secrets, pain, failures, and shame, the place where his great sadness and all his addictions were locked away.

When Paul's inner shack of addictions and shame was exposed, he realized he could either end it all, or step into relationship with God and others in a more authentic, transparent, and vulnerable way. He chose the long, slow, profound journey of openness and trust. He can say now of his relationship with God, "It is always face to face in the sense of open,

---

10. Young, "Wm. Paul Young," lines 42–49.

11. Robinson, "James Robinson and The Shack," lines 54–56.

12. Personal interview (3 July 2014).

13. Briere, *Child Abuse Trauma*, 49–56.

unashamed, and honest and authentic, and it is also always side by side, as in movement, journeying, adventure, participation."[14]

Paul credits his wife with saving his life by making him face himself and his inner demons. He found a Christian abuse counselor, Scott Mitchell, who took him through an intense nine months of therapy. But that was only the beginning. "It took eleven years," Paul says, "for our relationship to heal." Baxter Kruger, the theologian who wrote *The Shack Revisited*, observes: "eleven years of pain and emotional torture, depression, and mere flashes of hope—it was Kim's heroic love wrapped in fury that held it all together."[15]

DISCOVERING THE CHARACTER OF GOD: *THE SHACK*

In *The Shack*, Paul represents those eleven years of pain and depression through the weekend that Mack spends in the shack with Papa God. Though *The Shack* is a work of fiction, it "was born in the crucible of life, of trauma and abuse; of empty religion, misery and betrayal."[16]

After MacKenzie loses his daughter, he tries to maintain a semblance of faith in God, but underneath he believes there is no point in following a God who cannot—or chooses not—to save his little girl despite his desperate prayers. When he receives a note signed "Papa" (his wife's favorite name for God) inviting him to meet at the shack, the site of his daughter's murder, he doesn't know what to do. He doesn't believe God loves a "screwup like him. He was sick of God and God's religion."[17]

In spite of his doubt and confusion, he decides to visit the shack. Initially, no one seems to be there to meet him, which reinforces his belief in God's abandonment. Then Mack turns back to the shack to try again. This time:

> the door flew open, and he was looking directly into the face of a large, beaming African-American woman . . . [She] engulfed him in her arms, lifting him clear off his feet and spinning him around like a little child. And all the while she was shouting his name—"Mackenzie Allen Phillip"—with the ardor of someone seeing a long-lost and deeply loved relative . . . "Mack, look at you!" she

14. Ibid.
15. Kruger, *The Shack Revisited*, 8.
16. Ibid., 9.
17. Young, *The Shack*, 68.

fairly exploded. "Here you are, and so grown up. I have really been looking forward to seeing you face-to-face. It is so wonderful to have you here with us. My, my, my, how I do love you!"[18]

When Papa God explains why she is appearing to Mack as a woman, her reasons are clearly relevant for the author as well:

> "MacKenzie, I am neither male nor female, even though both genders are derived from my nature. If I choose to *appear* to you as a man or as a woman, it's because I love you. For me to appear to you as a woman and suggest that you call me 'Papa' is simply to mix metaphors, to keep from falling so easily back into your religious conditioning . . . To reveal myself to you as a very large, white grandfather figure with flowing beard, like Gandalf, would simply reinforce your religious stereotypes . . . Hasn't it always been a problem for you to embrace me as your Father? And after what you've been through, you couldn't very well handle a father right now, could you?"[19]

Then Mack meets the Holy Spirit, "a small distinctively Asian woman"[20] who seems to be a gardener and tells him she collects tears. "She seemed almost to shimmer in the light, and her hair blew in all directions even though there was hardly a breeze."[21] Then Jesus appears as a "Middle Eastern man and was dressed like a laborer, complete with tool belt and gloves . . . His features were pleasant enough, but he was not particularly handsome—not a man to stick out in a crowd. But his eyes and smile lit up his face, and Mack found it difficult to look away."[22]

As Mack tries to figure out who these people are, he wonders if "maybe this was a Trinity sort of thing. But two women and a man and none of them white? Then again, why had he naturally assumed that God would be white?"[23] He also encounters Sophia, Lady Wisdom of Proverbs, "a personification of Papa's wisdom."[24] He describes her as "A tall, beautiful, olive-skinned woman, with chiseled Hispanic features, clothed in a dark-colored

18. Ibid., 77.
19. Ibid., 95.
20. Ibid., 86.
21. Ibid.
22. Ibid.
23. Ibid., 89.
24. Ibid., 173.

flowing robe . . . regal as a high court judge,"[25] who helps him understand God's mercy and judgment.

Paul makes it clear that he does not depict God as female in his books in order to make a point about gender. Rather, he is interested in helping readers discover what God is truly like so that they will "see" God more accurately. As Papa God says in the previously quoted passage, coming as a bearded grandfather would only reinforce the religious stereotypes, including the concept of a punitive father. Thus the images are far less important than what they represent.

Throughout Paul's childhood, males sexually abused him, and his father was brutally angry with him. But at significant times along the way, women saw who he was and interacted with him. Women intercepted him when suicide was a real possibility. Given Paul's personal history, it is not surprising that he is drawn towards female imagery to represent the tenderness, acceptance, non-judgment, attentive care, and special fondness of God.

In reflecting on his relationship with God, Paul observes: "the trinity present themselves according to my need at the moment, they submit to who I am in the moment, sometimes I need a community, sometimes the nurturing listener, sometimes the big brother, sometimes a friend who knows me well, sometimes a father, sometimes a trusted mystery, sometimes a mother, the interplay of response to me and mine to them."[26] God's kindness and humility are demonstrated in this willingness to come to us in whatever way we need.

Paul's passion is for others to discover the profound acceptance of God and realize that they can trust God. He notes that we can't trust someone if we don't know that they love us, but "When we know we are loved, instead of seeking for something outside, we express from the inside out what is grounded in trust."[27]

UNCOVERING THE FACADE: CROSS ROADS

As Baxter Kruger observes in *The Shack Revisited*, "From a human perspective, without Kim and her heart, Paul Young would probably be dead,

---

25. Ibid., 154.
26. Personal email (7 July 2014).
27. Personal interview (3 July 2014).

tucked away in some cold asylum, or an empty man still performing."[28] This description of an empty man still performing is fitting for Tony Spencer, the self-centered protagonist of *Cross Roads*. Paul readily admits that his leading characters have a lot in common with himself—men who are all desperately in need of a God of grace.

In *Cross Roads*, Tony is admitted to an intensive care ward with a cerebral hemorrhage after severing himself from his family and living in paranoid isolation. While he is comatose, he begins a fantastical journey into his inner world—or is it the afterlife, he wonders—where he meets Jesus and the Holy Spirit.

Along with Paul Young and Mack, Tony could not have handled the image of God as a father either. In his anger, Tony asks, "So does this Father God live here . . . in my world?" He is told, "'He doesn't, not as a habitation anyway. Anthony you have never made a place for him, at least not inside these walls. While he is never absent, he also waits for you in the forest, outside the walls of your heart.'"[29]

On his inner journey, Tony becomes more familiar with the ramshackle homestead that is his own inner being, and he begins to see himself with new eyes as he gradually discovers the God who sees him with intense but unsentimental love. Tony meets "the Jesus person" first, who introduces him to "an elderly round woman, jet black hair falling in two braids," who is living in a hovel in the corner of the homestead property. "She wore a simple flowing calico dress, tightened by an ornate belt of more beads, and a sunburst starquilt blanket draped around her shoulders. Her eyes were closed, her face upturned. She was an Indian, a Native American or First Nations woman."[30] When Tony asks her who she is, she says:

> "Anthony, I am she who is more than you can begin to imagine and yet anchors your deepest longings. I am she whose love for you, you are not powerful enough to change, and I am she whom you can trust. I am the voice in the wind, the smile in the moon, the refreshing of the life that is water. I am the common wind that catches you by surprise and your very breath. I am fire and fury opposed to everything that you believe that is not Truth, that is hurting you and keeping you from being free."[31]

28. Kruger, *The Shack Revisited*, 8.

29. Young, *Cross Roads*, 80.

30. Ibid., 74.

31. Ibid., 92.

Tony's interactions with the Jesus person and the Holy Spirit alternate with encounters with people in his outer life, where he becomes able to see literally through the eyes of others. This experience draws him out of his intense self-centeredness. As he further explores his inner world, his growing awareness of his own brokenness helps him to realize how trapped he has been by painful events in his own life and his desperately selfish choices. In Tony's utter aloneness and despair, he hears a little girl's laughter and singing, and he finally prays for God's help. "[S]he was standing directly in front of him, perhaps all of six years old, raven hair tied back from smooth olive skin by a wreath of tiny white flowers, a white trillium tucked behind one ear. She had stunning brown eyes and was all smiles."[32] Though Tony doesn't recognize the little girl as God, "Her presence was like springtime unfolding, the thaw that warmed and invited new things. She stood directly in front of him, leaned in, and softly kissed his cheek . . . 'My name is Hope.' . . . 'I am the one who relentlessly loves you,' she said."[33]

Later, after Tony comes to accept this love that holds him, and to make some significant choices for the good of others, the Holy Spirit explains that the images that God uses in self-revelation are portals for us to perceive God more clearly. "Imagery," adds the grandmother figure, "has never been able to define God, but it is our intention to be known, and each whisper and breath of imagery is a little window into a facet of our nature."[34]

Throughout *Cross Roads*, the Trinity interact in mutual love and enjoyment of each other. As in *The Shack*, the focus is on character, rather than gender, as each meets the needs of the human person with whom they are interacting. This community of mutuality and love reflects something of Paul's early childhood among the Dani tribe. Of this experience, he writes:

> My memories of my young childhood within the tribe were foundational, no doubt. Like my mother I have no distinct memory of the presence of any Dani woman "in particular," that is, I had no one or two or few with whom my memory is attached. Unlike my mother, the presence of Dani women was ubiquitous, always present and surrounding. Perhaps this allowed me to be much more comfortable inside a presence of communal feminine embrace rather than having to form my attachments in particular.

32. Ibid., 198.
33. Ibid., 200.
34. Ibid., 286.

The imagery of the Trinity that were immediate to me would correspond well to this history.[35]

In reflecting on how his childhood has shaped his understanding of the Trinity, he says: "I talk to the trinity both communally and individually, there is a distinct sense of personhood with each and a comfortable awareness that even as I converse with one the three are present. It seems that I naturally relate to the Holy Spirit most easily in feminine form (probably a movement in part from 'it' theology to person theology)."[36]

In the early parts of *Cross Roads*, Tony loses his real self as he continues to perform vindictively, propping up "a facade in search of a heart."[37] Similarly, Paul observes that during his early years: "deeper than the issue of performance was the issue of 'being' itself, some proof that I existed. This relates to a phrase I have used quite often in the narrative—the facade (performance) was not an attempt at deception as much as it was hoping that if I performed perfectly, long enough, that presentation would become a 'real boy.' Perhaps, this is why the issues surrounding the commonality of our humanity, in part, touch me so much more than issues of gender."[38]

Paul's writing invites readers into that common humanity, the "being real" without facades, because we are known by a God who is especially fond of us, who loves us beyond our comprehension.

REVISITING THE CREATION STORY: *EVE*

Paul's life journey plays out in his writing and thinking, influencing his theological perspectives and understanding of God and humanness. In his third novel, *Eve*, he tackles questions around the nature of temptation and sin (turning from God), the nature of God, and issues of gender and gender relationships. He offers a stark reinterpretation of the biblical account of Genesis 1–3 to provoke readers to examine their assumptions—such as Adam being created as an adult, Eve being the first to sin, and God being masculine and punitive. While the reinterpretation will be considered heretical by some readers, Paul uses the gaps in the text to tell a story which will stimulate thought and discussion.

---

35. Personal email (9 July 2014).
36. Personal email (10 July 2014).
37. Young, *Cross Roads*, 5.
38. Personal email (10 July 2014).

The fictional story centers around a fifteen-year-old girl, Lilly Fields, who has been trafficked, lost at sea, and cast up on an island between this world and the next. As she is nursed back to health, she meets spiritual beings and discovers that she has been chosen to be a witness to the creation of the world (and the Genesis story). As in his two previous books, Paul paints Creator God as an interaction of three persons—Adonai, the Eternal Man, and *Ruach*, the breath of God. And again, as in *The Shack* and *Cross Roads*, God is constantly loving, consistently drawing us back into relationship—yet respecting our choices—and discovering ways to help us know how deeply we are loved. Lilly, as a representative of all humanity, has been deeply wounded psychologically, sexually, physically, and spiritually. Her healers reflect God's kindness and gentleness, while also understanding her fear and self-alienation.

At the beginning of *Eve*, one of Lilly's healers meets the timeless Eve, who (like Mother Eve in MacDonald's *Lilith*) is herself a representative of the Divine feminine: "The tall, fine-boned, ebony-black woman accepted his silent invitation and settled next to him, her hand tousling the grayblack hair at the back of his neck with the tenderness of a mother toward her child . . . Coarse white hair formed a woven crown around her face, lined and creased by countless years, a masterpiece of sculpted joy and sorrow. She glowed more like a child than a matriarch, her mahogany eyes lit by expectancy."[39]

Eve also meets with Lilly and tells her she is to be a witness to the creation of the cosmos. Lilly recounts her understanding of the creation story: "'God makes the world perfect, God makes man, God makes woman, woman ruins everything . . . everyone has been mad at women ever since.'"[40] But slowly, her understanding changes as she is invited to see the unfolding story of our beginnings: the big bang, the creation of the earth, and the birth of Adam, brought forth from the earth: "Adonai sang into it and then with tears and laughter plunged His hands into the holy mess with a shout that brought Lilly to her feet. The labor was nearly finished. Then, with a piercing, wrenching scream, Adonai raised above His head a newborn baby . . . The crystal-clear and gentle voice of Eternal Man now sang above the cacophony: 'This is My heart's delight, the crowning of all

39. Young, *Eve*, 1, 2.
40. Ibid., 27.

creation. I present to you My beloved son, in whom My soul delights. They shall be named Adam!'"[41]

So Adam is born a baby and fed at the breasts of God. When Lilly questions her care-giver about this, he answers: "Of course They have breasts, and full of milk according to the Scriptures. Mother's milk."[42]

As the Genesis story continues, Lilly sees Adam's temptation and his turning from God to believe the serpent. The result of his turning is that he experiences alienation from God and believes himself alone, even when Adonai is right beside him. He longs for a face-to-face relationship, seeking this in naming the animals. But this is a pointless task, as one of the healers later explains to Lilly: "'if one is seeking a face-to-face relationship, naming is a futile exercise. Dominion cannot carry you there. There was no counterpart in all creation for Adam, and God patiently let him prove it.'"[43] In God's goodness, he creates Eve, born from Adam's body, to be one with whom he can relate face-to-face:

> In nine months God fashioned the feminine side of Adam's humanity, the female who slept within, into a breathtaking being of corresponding power but weak and fragile as the source from which she was withdrawn . . . then she was taken out of the he, one separating into two. No longer would either ever be the all, and yet Adonai promised that by Love's knowing, the two could one day choose to celebrate as one. The wide expanse of God's one nature was now expressed in two, the female and the male, both by nature designed to live face-to-face with Father, Son, and Spirit.[44]

Thus both Adam and Eve, male and female, can relate to God fully. For man, the woman is a reminder to know his own weakness and need for the other. "She is Adonai's invitation to embrace frailty and softness, to be whole and unashamed, to return fully from his turning."[45] And while this male-female relationship creates the possibility for wholeness, in itself it is not enough. Only relationship with the Divine Other is enough. As Adonai explains, Adam turns "to the ground for security and worth, identity and meaning, though it cannot give what it does not have."[46] Eve turns to Adam

41. Ibid., 34, 35.

42. Ibid., 142.

43. Ibid., 156–57.

44. Ibid., 187.

45. Ibid., 188.

46. Ibid., 244.

for her meaning, and although there is indeed a turning away from God in this, there is still something of goodness. For as Mother Eve explains to Lilly: "Perhaps this desire to reach out to the other, to make amends and repair loss, to build a bridge and heal, is a part of God's maternal being that is in all of us. Womb-love, mercy!"[47]

In Paul's first two novels, the Creator and the Holy Spirit within the Trinity are represented as two female beings, and Jesus is depicted as a man. In *Eve*, God is more clearly both male and female. Yet the story line interprets Eve herself to be part of God's invitation to Adam to re-turn (to come back into face-to-face relationship), suggesting that the feminine is more relational, perhaps even more whole.

Paul's own life experiences have caused him to reflect deeply on the nature of sin and the power of wounding. By sharing his profound healing journey and his encounters with a masculine-feminine God whose utterly unchanging love woos the most broken person back into relationship, Paul invites others into their own healing journeys. His novels beckon readers to re-examine their assumptions about the relationship between men and women as well as their relationships with a God who is both masculine and feminine—and who is unfailingly devoted to us.

MIDLIFE JOURNEY: TOWARDS CHILDLIKENESS, BALANCE AND FREEDOM

Many men in Western culture can identify with Paul's sense that he had become a "performer"—someone who was trying to prove to the world that he was a "real person," that he had what it takes, that he could succeed, that he was worthwhile. As Henri Nouwen writes, "It is not success, achievement, pride that are the major problems. It is self-rejection. And we hear the voice that says—Go on prove yourself—Prove you are good enough."[48]

The major turning point in Paul's life came when he realized that he had tried everything he knew to "measure up" and had failed miserably. As Baxter Kruger observes, "He performed himself into ministry, into business, into marriage, into fatherhood, trying to the point of exhaustion to become an authentic human being while hiding the underlying shame and personal failures."[49] Baxter goes on to explain how the poison of shame can

47. Ibid., 282.
48. Nouwen, *Life of the Beloved*, 31.
49. Kruger, *The Shack Revisited*, 8.

cause people to "turn to another person, a 'magical other' who will be our all in all, our life, our salvation."[50]

Paul's journey exemplifies Carl Jung's description of the midlife process of integration. Using Scriptures, myths, and stories as windows into the human condition, Jung cites a passage from the third-century story of the Shepherd of Hermas to convey how the feminine can become not only erotic but divine: "Now, while I prayed, the heaven was opened, and I see the lady, whom I had desired, greeting me from heaven."[51] Jung explains that when men repress their erotic desire, they activate the "image of the goddess, i.e., the archetypal soul-image,"[52] which is woman as mother and woman as desirable maid. These images "have immense power, as they release forces, both in the child and in the adult man," which can be named accurately as divine because they are so "irresistible and absolutely compelling."[53]

Paul honestly admits that the fantasies he had about his affair were messianic, and he saw his relationship with "the other woman" as compelling and divine. "The adultery was about the imagination of what she represented. I literally stepped outside boundaries of reality. I believed that somehow we were going to save the world."[54] Jung explains how the idolatrous illusion must be exposed and dashed to pieces, forcing the man to face his real humanity so that he can engage in the deep work of integration, combining the head and heart, the feminine and masculine, within himself. When "man is forced to his knees before the divine image . . . He is restored to himself again and, flung back on himself, finds himself once more between gods and men, following his own path."[55]

However, in the face of this inner division, if man continues to seek wholeness outside of himself, he is vulnerable to unfaithfulness. But if he can remain committed to the deep journey of honesty, to the pain of the awareness of his inner disintegration, the healthy desire for wholeness can culminate in a more fully integrated self. "This is what happens very frequently about the midday of life, and in this wise our miraculous human nature enforces the transition that leads from the first half of life to the

---

50. Ibid.

51. "The Shepherd of Hermas," 1:4.

52. Jung, "Aspects of the Feminine," 10.

53. Ibid.

54. Personal interview (3 July 2014).

55. Jung, "Aspects of the Feminine," 10.

second. It is a metamorphosis . . . a transformation of nature into culture, of instinct into spirit."[56]

Richard Rohr, who is introduced in chapter 5, follows Jung, but describes the male spiritual journey as a transformation from a wild man to wise man.[57] Rohr explains that it is important for men to recognize both the negative and the positive in the male soul: *the way to transmute the pain of life is to reveal the wounded side of all things, and then place the wound inside sacred space.*[58] He points out that the biblical stories contain violence, adulteries, injustice, betrayals. "It is about naming, facing and forgiving the wounds of history, which is quite different than excluding them, denying them, or making them impossible."[59] The deliberate inclusion of the negative, he says, is an important part of the meaning of the crucifixion. "You cannot contain evil by shaming it, but only by revealing it for what it is and then seeing the good as better . . . A man who owns his limitations and weeps over his sin is much more effective than one who thinks he has neither."[60]

In clarifying the male journey, Richard Rohr—similar to Jung before him—names midlife as the crisis of limitation. He describes the first half of life as the "heroic journey." But when the man discovers that the rules don't work any more, he can continue to attempt the heroic journey of ascent, or he can become embittered, or he can face his limitations, his wounds, and his shadow and choose instead to embrace the wisdom journey.[61]

This is the journey that Paul made when he began to engage with his emotions and the parts of himself that he had shut down when he projected his longing for the Divine onto another human being through his affair. By choosing the path of vulnerability and transparency and by engaging his woundedness rather than hiding his shame, secrets, failures, and addictions in his metaphorical shack, he began the work of integrating the head and the heart and the masculine and the feminine within himself. His journey now is leading him into greater wholeness, further childlikeness, and more expansive freedom in his relationship with the Triune God, others, and himself.

56. Ibid., 49.
57. Rohr, *From Wild Man to Wise Man.*
58. Rohr, *Adam's Return,* 117 (italics in original).
59. Ibid.
60. Ibid., 118.
61. Rohr, *From Wild Man to Wise Man,* 166–67.

9

Captivating God
Ordinary people and the Divine Feminine

This is a story about the miraculous opening of my heart, the descent into the power and love of the Divine Feminine, and the discovery of how to deeply love a woman.[1]

My own encounter with God as mother and as lover has been a long and slowly developing journey through which I have come to experience healing. Though I have wanted to share these ways of engaging God with others, I have been aware that men experience this process differently. Journeying with men and women in spiritual companioning or spiritual direction enables people to honestly and vulnerably explore their perceptions of God. William Barry, a long time spiritual director, and prolific writer about spirituality and relationship with God, has noticed how people's images of God change over time. He notes, "As we develop our relationship with God, experience shows what parts of our images are analogous to the real God, what parts are distortions of the real God. In the course of that development some people find that at least for a time the image of God becomes feminine. It seems the only way that God can convince us that she/he is beyond gender categorization and that masculinity is not the favored

---

1. Dorsett, *Journey to a Woman's Heart*, 24.

gender."[2] He continues that our old images of God "can be sources of resistance to the development of our relationship with God. It has happened that a new development in relationship has been slowed or resisted because the person involved became frightened or anxious at the gender shift God seemed to be making. All our images of God are in some sense idols which ultimately want to imprison God. Perhaps the strongest idol is the image of God as male."[3]

One of the resistances we have to the perception of God as feminine is the struggle we have with eros, the bringing together of agape love and erotic love in our understanding of God. Many Christians think that eros and agape should be kept separate, because they define agape as the love of a holy God, whereas eros is earthy, sexual, and even sinful. Some Christians identify the body as secular and the spirit as sacred, whereas others reclaim the truth of the incarnation, affirming that God is at home in the body, and eros is the vitality of all of life. Father Ronald Rolheiser writes: "Spirituality concerns what we do with desire. It takes its root in the eros inside of us and it is all about how we shape and discipline that eros. John of the Cross, the great Spanish mystic, begins his famous treatment of the soul's journey with the words: 'One dark night, fired by love's urgent longings.' For him it is urgent longings, eros, that are the starting points of the spiritual life and, in his view, spirituality."[4] In this poem "Dark Night," John of the Cross identifies himself with the feminine beloved. C. S. Lewis argues that all men are in some way feminine before God, since God is the active agent.[5] Although these responses may be more representative of another time, they illustrate one possible way that men can understand their journey with God. Other men respond to this longing for intimacy by encountering the feminine Divine.

As I have engaged with these various perspectives and prayerfully sought God, I have also asked friends about their encounters with God and their awareness of gender. One friend offers the following perspective:

> Firstly, I am a man, husband, father, son, brother of Christ, disciple
> of Christ, man among men and brother to/of many, and there is
> a 'homo-erotic' aspect to this (although I've chosen not to enter

2. Barry, *God and You*, 38.

3. Ibid.

4. Rolheiser, *The Holy Longing*, 7.

5. Lewis, *The Problem of Pain*, 44. "Our role must be always that of patient to agent, female to male, mirror to light, echo to voice."

into a homosexual experience with anyone). I seek to explore and penetrate the mystery, spiritually and sexually. My spiritual modus operandi reflects my sexual design. However, secondly, there is another side to me that says I surrender, I am receptive, penetrate me, take me. I am learning to wait for the mystery (sometimes) rather than always be out there hunting it down! And then, thirdly, there are times when the question of gender all but disappears in favour of simple shared humanity. Not that I become neutered, or anyone else for that matter, but at times it ceases to matter.[6]

Some of the men whose perspectives frame the previous chapters have led rather extraordinary lives. Thus their encounters with God may seem foreign or distant to many readers. Therefore, in this chapter, I have collected stories from contemporary Christian men whose longings to know God truly and deeply have led them to encounter the feminine Divine. While their stories reflect the challenge of these encounters, their lives have all been touched by the experience of relating to the feminine in God.

ENCOUNTERING GOD AS MOTHER

Because I have become convinced that relating with God as both mother and father, lover and friend is necessary for the fullness of life, I have begun to include this perspective in my counseling classes. In this section, I include responses from three Asian students who have participated in my postgraduate classes and have discovered this new way of encountering God as a revelation. They reflect on how their relationships with God were affected by their relationships with their parents, especially the sternness, or distance, of their fathers. All were relieved to discover that what they had experienced in their relationships with their mothers was also possible with God.

Alain (Philippines)

Alain is involved in ministry and counseling as well as research around sexual orientation. His response to encountering God as mother shows his awareness of how powerfully gender interacts with pictures of God. He writes: "Another striking thing for me in this class was the revelation the Lord has shown me about God as a mother too! Truly I was happy that my

6. Alexander, "God and Gender," 112.

heart was filled with joy when He made me realize that He can be a Father and a Mother when I need him!"[7]

Having studied counseling, Alain is very aware that his childhood relationships, especially with his father, have an impact on his image of God, and he has journeyed deeply with God the Father in a healing relationship. He explains:

> I grew up with a disengaged relationship to my earthly father and I believe it has somehow affected my view of God the Father especially before my life in Christ. For me He was simply up in heaven watching over me, looking at how am I doing whether good or bad, and ready to chastise when I fail or have sinned. This is somewhat how I also delineate my father, a provider, and head of the family who loves us, his children, from a distance. Of course, this view has changed when I started to know more of God as I journey with Jesus. But I have to say that there were times that it was difficult for me to utter the word "Father." Whenever I pray or sing songs of praise with this word, a picture of my father comes into my mind . . . This was one major issue that God has worked in me as I have got to know Him more through His words, teachings, and His self-revelation to me![8]

As Alain engaged with the possibility that he could respond to God as a mother, not just a father, he suddenly found another way to encounter God that would deepen his trust and his ability to receive God's love.

> And today, I am finally recognizing like a light shining very brightly, that yes God is also God the Mother! It dawned on me, and now I comprehend fully in the of light those verses, at last, the ones that describe how a mother nurtures or loves her child, like Isaiah 42:14, 49:15, Jeremiah 31:20, Psalm 22:9–10 among others, that these also describe the characteristics of God as a loving and nurturing Mother! This experience for me was like "Wow! That was it!" and made me feel that I can more fully depend on and trust our motherly and fatherly God![9]

---

7. Alain, Personal communication.

8. Ibid

9. Ibid.

Timothy (Central Asia)

Timothy, who is involved in ministry in Central Asia, has also been impacted by the parenting style of his father. Because Timothy has struggled to approach his father, he has had difficulty approaching Father God. At first, he struggled to address God as mother because he had never heard of this possibility. Nevertheless, he persisted, and he explains how he experienced the warmth of God's love for the first time:

> At first I was cautious when you suggested we try addressing God as "Mother God" in one of the classes. I felt very uncomfortable even trying to utter this simple word. I have heard and seen people addressing God as father and friend, but "Mother"—not even once in my whole life and it was the first time that I have heard something like this. Even though I could relate better and I am closer with my mother than my father, still addressing God as mother was so hard. Despite this I continuously tried to address God as mother. It was a very nice feeling, I could feel the warmth and care of the motherly love and I felt closer addressing him as mother rather than father. I think this is because I have seen my own dad who was very strict and bossy, so I never felt close whenever I addressed God as father. For the first time I felt that warmth in God's love. Yes, our society being male dominated always sees God as some kind of fatherly figure; a dominant one, all powerful and at times seeming very unapproachable and a really strict God. So was my case before, since my earthly father was very strict and disciplined. Addressing him as mother was a very unique and lovely way to connect to God.[10]

Archie (Philippines)

Archie is also involved in ministry and pastoral care, and he speaks about the challenge of addressing God as mother:

> I entered Bible College in 2009 with a basic understanding on the *basics* of the faith. It was completely new to me to hear and openly see God in His motherly love and care—He, being a *Mother God*. I honestly struggled. My limited mind was barely groping in this absolutely new concept of understanding the unfathomable and unlimited God that I know. I remained open with my accumulated

---

10. Timothy, personal communication.

convictions right at the corner of my head, while allowing this new truth to percolate its way to my being.[11]

After carefully evaluating whether or not he should come to God as mother, Archie "never chanced upon any contradicting issues in my faith and walk with God," and so he ventured into the encounter described below.

> Liberating and absolutely helpful are the words I have, to define the result of entertaining and eventually embracing this truth about my God. In fact, His images whenever I think of Him, visualize Him in different situations, and more so during my prayer times, have been powerful enough to affirm His nearness, attendance and warmth towards me. This is not to undermine the fatherly figure of God. My life experiences perhaps would attest to my personal responses to this.[12]

In contrast to Alain and Timothy, Archie had a very loving relationship with his father, but his father had to work elsewhere, and so his mother provided continuity of love:

> I had rich memories of my childhood. I was bathed with love and support and early realities about life and the challenges circling around it. Most of my intermediary years were spent with my mama alone watching over us three siblings, while papa worked in another province and would only come home to spend the weekends with us. Those were blissful and remarkable days of true happiness for me to experience their presence, especially mealtimes on a Saturday night. I had valid longings and high anticipations during weekends. Being the firstborn in the family, I looked up to papa's leadership and desired to be like him someday. I would cherish the good old days when he would teach me weekly the basics of guitar and *banduria* on top of singing a Filipino nursery song, "Pen Pen De Sarapen." These gradually changed as the years passed, the mentoring moments ebbed due to his employment requirements. However, one thing lingered. Mama remained providing us her warm and loving parental care and I must say, it was her doting ministries to us that brought us to where we are right now—God-fearing and responsible individuals in facing the beauty and challenges of life.[13]

11. Archie, personal communication.
12. Ibid.
13. Ibid.

Over time, Archie began to use his God-given imagination and knowledge of the Scriptures to encounter God as an intimate and loving mother.

> My appreciation of my foundational experience of love is being brought to the surface as I get to cuddle the image of my Mother God who takes delight in putting me in her lap, satisfies my longing for food and nutrients through her life-giving milk from her breast. A Mother God who widely opens her wings to invite me to come and wrap me in that protective and reassuring presence. Indeed, God is a relational God. He is a connecting Deity. The omnipotent Creator and sustainer of the Heavens and the earth is the same God who enjoys my fellowship with Him. Regardless of His gender, He is very particular with me. He takes delight in me. He makes Himself available and to be drawn to for as long as I desire Him in my life. His mystery will always be a mystery. The dynamics of His character (and gender character) will forever be unsearchable and unlimited.[14]

These three men have been touched by God in new ways as they have opened themselves to relating to the maternal biblical images for God. Though this concept was new, they entrusted themselves to a faithful God who would correct, reveal, and lead them into deeper knowing.

ENCOUNTERING GOD AS EROTIC LOVER

James, a Christian from a conservative tradition, has been involved in ministry and spiritual accompaniment for many years.[15] Though he enjoyed a stable and happy marriage, he longed for more intimacy with God. Earlier in his spiritual journey, James needed to experience a father-child relationship with God in order to heal his own father wound: "my soul needed to hear words from God—words from a father. It was important that I heard and deeply owned Father God's words to me: 'You, my child, are absolutely loved; I really am proud of you. You have a voice that the world needs to hear.'"

As this healing settled, God invited James to greater freedom, whispering:

> Come, explore with me; come, explore me! For your whole life, explore me! An image came to me—more like a video clip. It was

14. Archie, personal communication.

15. The story that follows is drawn from his personal communication with me.

of me on a dance floor having a go at some uninhibited free-form dance moves and falling flat on my face! God comes over, and with a wonderful belly laugh, puts out his hand to help me to my feet, inviting me to try again. I remember at that moment feeling wonderfully relieved, being aware that some kind of weight had fallen off me, knowing that it's all right to make some theological blunders along the way in this journey, that it's not fatal.

This invitation from God to explore, to dance, and to trust God even in mistakes opened the door to encounters James had not expected as he was awakened to God through dreams and images. "One night I had a dream. Two archetypal females were central—the Wise Woman and the Wild Woman. In the dream the Wise Woman directed me to go to the Wild Woman. I think it was the indwelling Holy Spirit saying, 'Now it's time to get to know other sides of me.' It felt remarkably liberating."

The freedom that came from these encounters enabled James to respond to the surprise of the feminine Holy Spirit. He describes his discoveries about this "wild feminine:"

> . . . not simply the encapsulation of God's energy or life force, but a person, an intriguing, captivating person, and definitely female in nature! The secret name by which I now love to address her is "Wild Lover Grace." She beckons, she invites, she entices, she captivates, she tantalizes, she delights, she fascinates, she seduces me . . . It is eros love, and it touches deeply into my male desire. Yes, absolutely, it visits my sexuality . . . the energy it releases is freeing, it is creative, and it is life-giving. And it has opened me to wonderful moments of intimacy with my God . . . Wild Woman Grace refuses to be domesticated. She is edgy, playful and unpredictable. She cannot be contained indoors. She entices me into wide spaces without walls; she is a woman of the outdoors.

James's encounter with the feminine Divine came during a retreat. After praying to see her face, "What resulted was a sense of a face, beautiful but also showing the signs of some age and some exposure to the weather. It had been a very, very special experience but I longed for more." He particularly wanted to experience her gaze, and he experienced more later while on a six-day silent retreat. He recounts:

> What happened was totally unpredictable: a sense of a female presence, her face slowly coming closer and closer to mine. I felt drawn however, not to her eyes, but to her mouth—her lips—now very close to my cheek. I felt a deep sense of intimacy. Her mouth

moved towards mine; it seemed like only a centimetre or two away. I was anticipating her kiss, but it was not to be. Her lips parted and slowly and gently she breathed her breath into my mouth. Then I was gently exhaling and my breath was being received into her mouth. It was like it happened in slow motion and it felt like it easily fell into a rhythm, she breathing into my mouth, me into hers, and she, so close. I remember wanting this to go on and on, wanting it never to stop. It felt like absolute intimacy.

In his journal, he wrote: "She is Beauty. She is Eros Love . . . We are one. Then I hear her unspoken thought for me: 'Our breath is prayer.' She is praying into me. I am returning her prayer. I know in my deepest part: This is what I was born for! . . . Tears come. And I know that this is far from just imagination; it carries power and freedom. More than anything, it visits my deepest longing."

While this powerful encounter with God touched the deepest parts of James's being, he recalls how quickly he questioned the reality of the experience: "That afternoon I fell into the darkest hours of doubt of my entire life. Were these things I had recently been experiencing really just the product of my own psychic maladies—my own need to create a reality to satisfy my neuroses?"

As he prayed and wrestled with his questions he found a way forward, making a choice of faith: "The end of that darkness was marked by a remarkable sense of affirmation in my spirit and my mind: 'I choose to believe this season in my faith is indeed the reality of who I am in God. Why? Because through this season I have known life and freedom as I have never experienced it before. I am choosing to actually, for the rest of my life, live and die on the reality of this!'"

James's story demonstrates God's responsiveness to us and willingness to lead us into deeper intimacy as we each answer God's invitation. His journey of healing as an unfolding relationship with the Divine parallels the following story from Bob, whose experience with the Divine feminine brought about a blossoming of authentic human sexual relationships.

INTIMACY WITH THE DIVINE FEMININE, INTIMACY WITH OTHERS

In *Journey to a Woman's Heart*, Bob Dorsett uses poetry and reflection to trace his spiritual longing and his engagement with eros, a journey that eventually freed him to love. He grew up in Catholic schools and then en- tered seminary, being taught that girls were off-limits and that if he left the seminary he would be choosing "an inferior life."[16] After seminary, he was ordained and vowed to "never experience human sexual love."[17] Of that vow, he writes: "This was a lifetime promise I made in the Catholic Church when I was ordained a priest at twenty-five years of age, a vow that requires that I be cautious in my closeness to women and give up the sacred human love that can grow from that closeness."[18]

Several years after his ordination, he slowly developed a loving, then sexual, relationship with a nun. During this time, he noticed that he be- came more human and gracious with his parishioners, but he also felt very guilty. He recalls:

> I continued my love relationship, and two voices continued to wage war within me, the voice of guilt and the voice of love. Which one was I going to follow? Looking back on those days, there really was no contest. The voice of my heart, although silenced for years in the catacomb of guilt, spoke the truth, and the voice of guilt, deeply embedded and programmed into my head, was reduced to a mere whisper . . . Since then, I have been undoing years of negative programming and climbing the mountain of the sacred path of human love.[19]

Bob left the priesthood and discontinued the sexual relationship, real- izing that he needed much healing. He went to counseling, participated in workshops, and read many books, especially Carl Jung. He began to recog- nize, as Jung did, that for a man the journey to maturity is an interwoven journey of discovering his own masculine and feminine, of finding the feminine in the Divine, and of relating to women authentically. In retro- spect, Bob realized how immature he was in his relationships.

While learning to become a more authentically whole person, he married a woman with whom he always seemed to agree. Because he chose a path of accommodation rather than the true self, his marriage was short-lived. But when his wife first left him, he was unable to recognize the problems. He concludes, "Through my searching and my mistakes, I began to suspect that when human love comes from the heart, it is the full

16. Dorsett, *Journey to a Woman's Heart*, 11.
17. Ibid., 11.
18. Ibid., 11.
19. Ibid., 16–17.

expression of Divine love and is just as sacred. I also unwittingly discovered that to express sacred love to a woman, I first needed to discover and learn to embrace the sacred feminine within myself, and, through her, to re-discover the depths of my own sacred masculine."[20]

As part of that masculine journey, Bob travelled, climbed mountains, and explored wild places. But after a time, one of his counselors remarked that though his exploration of the masculine was important, maybe now he needed to explore the feminine within. Bob realized that there was a deep connection between finding the feminine within, finding the way to the authentic heart of a woman, and also responding to the Divine feminine. He reflects: "To experience the Divine, I need to be fully human. Therefore, to be whole, I need to feel sacred love for a woman as a heart-centered sexual man. When I experience heart-centered love with a woman, I discover that the human in me is connected to the Divine; in fact, they become one."[21]

As Bob continued to seek God and to discover the depths of God's love and also to become more honest with himself and others, he was able to develop a more mature relationship with a woman. At this point, he was more fully himself, relating to another who could be fully herself, and in this way he held both the internal and external feminine.

In Bob's journey, we witness the intertwining of human love and sexuality with encounters with the feminine Divine. Bob observes: "I have journeyed into the consciousness of the Divine feminine and discovered that her presence and her power are real. This journey has awakened in me not only a profound respect and love for women, but also a deep knowing of the joy of discovering the fullness of my masculine . . . This is not a theoretical construct that I have solely studied; it is a reality that I have personally experienced."[22]

Bob Dorsett's story traces the difficult journey of revelation, which was sparked by his reaction to religious legalism. Like the men discussed in earlier chapters, he made mistakes along the way, hurt other people, and needed slow healing and painful honesty and self-revelation to discover an authentic romantic and sexual relationship and to experience the joy of freedom.

20. Ibid., 17.

21. Ibid., 11.

22. Ibid., 24.

SPIRITUAL COMPANION FOR THE JOURNEY

Both James and Bob mentioned the importance of someone walking beside them in the deep places of their spiritual journey. The Christian faith has a long tradition of recognizing a spiritual companion or soul friend to help guide us in our walk with God, especially when the way is dark or our revelations unusual, or our discernments challenging. The early Celts recognized the importance of an *anam cara* as they called the soul friend, Bridget of Ireland (451–525) even declaring that a person without a soul friend was like a body without a head.

This practice of one believer helping another on the spiritual journey has a centuries-long tradition, one that has developed into formalized "spiritual direction" relationships which focus on the person's experience of God. Long-time spiritual directors William Barry and William Connolly define spiritual direction as helping the person to "pay attention to God's personal communication to him or her, to respond to this personally communicating God, to grow in intimacy with this God, and to live out the consequences of the relationship."[23]

When James experienced "the darkest hours of doubt" on his retreat he asked his spiritual director to help him discern whether his experience was truly God's communication with him. He was aware his own neuroses could be influencing him. Mortals need the wisdom of others to clarify what is from God and what is from ourselves. In chapter 1 Sandra Schneiders spoke of the need of healing for our images of God: "What must be undertaken is a therapy of the religious imagination."[24] Spiritual directors are skilled in this healing process, accompanying the believer in the delicate work of the Spirit's transforming of distortions of God-images, and daring to trust God's revelation of love and intimacy.

CONCLUSION

Each of the men in this chapter have encountered God in unique ways as they have opened themselves to God and trusted in God's faithfulness. The God of surprise has drawn them to relate more deeply and fully, bringing them wholeness. As Ronald Rolheiser writes, "Sexuality lies at the centre of the spiritual life. A healthy sexuality is the single most powerful vehicle

23. Barry and Connolly, *The Practice of Spiritual Direction*, 8.
24. Schneiders, *Women and the Word*, 19.

there is to lead us to selflessness and joy."[25] The experiences of the men who have shared their stories in this chapter reflect how sexuality and the sacred come together and how ordinary Christian men can relate to God both as mother and as female lover.

25. Rolheiser, *Seeking Spirituality*, 182.

Conclusion

The Ongoing Journey

In a word, SHE WHO IS discloses in an elusive female metaphor the mystery of Sophia-God as sheer, exuberant, relational aliveness in the midst of the history of suffering, inexhaustible source of new being in situations of death and destruction, ground of hope for the whole created universe.[1]

In the introduction, I wondered about the difference it might make if a child grew up hearing both masculine and feminine names for God. In the journey towards adulthood, how might that child's sense of self be different? Perhaps our children or our grandchildren will answer that question. Perhaps they will be able to tell us from experience who they are discovering God to be—and the fuller sense they have as a result of that journey.

The men who shared their stories in the previous chapters point toward the difference it has made for them to experience a feminine God in adulthood. In this conclusion, I will review some of the key developments as a way of inviting us to revisit our experiences in the hope that we might hear from the God who is both male and female and simultaneously beyond gender. May that journey bring us to more fullness of being as we respond to stirrings from the Divine One, who created us and calls us forth in love.

---

1. Johnson, *She Who Is*, 243.

MOTHER GOD

The second verse of Genesis depicts the image of a feminine spirit whose wings overshadow the earth. This image of the overshadowing, loving God, who keeps us safe under her wings, reappears throughout the Bible, notably in the Psalms and Isaiah, as well as in Jesus' longing to gather the people of Jerusalem like a hen gathering her chicks under her wings. This image of a brooding feminine spirit reappears in the early centuries in Syriac Christianity, and the writings of the church fathers and mystics depict feminine images for all persons of the Trinity.

The character of this loving, feminine God appears consistently in the works of the other writers mentioned in this book. The Moravian Count Zinzendorf (1700–1760) spoke of the Holy Spirit as the Mother who comforts and gives life. George MacDonald's feminine God figures are often depicted with eyes which touch the soul: "They filled me with an unknown longing . . . I looked deeper and deeper, till they spread around me like seas, and I sank in their waters."[2] In MacDonald's works, the Divine mother figure ultimately offers safety and deep security, even though the journey may be difficult or dangerous. Commenting about George MacDonald, Kerry Dearborn writes, "MacDonald's desire to write and preach about God emerged from a passionate love and adoration of God. God was not a distant reality to be examined, but a beloved Father/Mother (of both strength and tenderness) whom he wanted all to meet."[3] For Thomas Merton, the mother figure was Mary, the Queen of Heaven, who cared for him even when he was wayward and thought there was no God. In *The Shack*, Paul Young describes the delight of the black Mother God meeting Mack again after a long time of absence. Timothy, the Asian student we meet in chapter 9, simply tried talking to Mother God and suddenly found God very close. Similarly, the Filipino students Alain and Archie encountered a new warmth and closeness with God when they opened their hearts to the possibility that God was like their mothers. These consistent experiences of the Mother God bear witness to the movement of the Spirit and echo the words from Isaiah: "Even these [a mother] may forget, yet I will not forget you, I have inscribed you on the palms of my hands" (Isa 49:15–16).

In my own journey, I experienced a deeper engagement with Mother God during an extended silent retreat. My personal experiences of giving

2. MacDonald, *Phantastes*, 45.

3. Dearborn, *Baptized Imagination*, 173.

birth and breast-feeding helped me connect with my deep, instinctual delight in my sons. When I accepted this spontaneous, profound love and willingness to sacrifice anything in caring for my children, my experience of God's mother love for me deepened.

When my sons were small, we had a single mother come and live with us for a time. Her own father had been alcoholic, and she struggled in her relationships with men. As she saw my husband playing with our sons, she glimpsed something of the love of the Father God she had not seen through her own childhood experiences. Her responses helped me to see how ordinary life experiences, such as watching parent-child relationships, can heal us and open us to receive from God the love that has always been present, but may have been veiled. For when we glimpse the mother-love or father-love of God, a window opens through which we can receive the love we may have missed out on, whether natural or supernatural.

Thus when we come to know God as both mother and father, we experience a fuller and more intimate expression of God's love. Rather than expecting judgment from God, we are more ready to receive God's loving care and correction.

GOD AS LOVER

Many men struggle with images of romantic, erotic, divine love. Yet as Rowan Williams reminds us in "The Body's Grace," "the joy created in committed sexual relationships helps us to understand what it is to desire God and be desired by God, as we have experienced desiring and being desired by another person."[4] Perhaps women can more readily identify with the beloved in the Song of Songs or with Mary Magdalene's relationship with Jesus. Even though men across the centuries have used erotic and sensual love language to describe God, these have tended to be hidden gems rather than obvious invitations. In speaking to the Divine lover, John Donne writes, "nor ever chaste unless you ravish me." St. John of the Cross speaks of laying his head on his Divine Lover's breast. We also see a lover-beloved relationship with the Divine in St. Francis's devotion to Lady Poverty.

In *Phantastes*, George MacDonald demonstrates the male journey of discovering spirituality and wisdom through a romantic search. Thomas Merton and Paul Young both reveal how their real-life romances, however misguided, eventually led them to deeper intimacy with God. Bob Dorsett

4. Cornwall, *Theology and Sexuality*, 30.

specifically connects his journey with the Divine feminine to his learning how to love a woman deeply. James's surprising invitation from the Wild Woman led to his profound encounter with the Divine feminine, the God of the Bible, She who is.

Many of us have been wounded by our intimate relationships. Yet God is inviting us into deeper wholeness by seeking to relate to all of our personhood—spiritual, emotional, and sexual. My hope is that as you read and continue to ponder these stories, you may find further courage to respond to the God who says, "I am your father, your mother, your brother, your sister, your lover, and your spouse."[5]

5. Nouwen, *Life of the Beloved*, 11.

Bibliography

Alexander, Irene. "God and Gender: The Relational Center." In *Reconsidering Gender: Evangelical Perspectives,* edited by Myk Habets and Beulah Wood, 116–34. Eugene, OR: Pickwick, 2010.

Ambrose. "Letter 41: The Synagogue at Callinicum." In *Early Latin Theology,* edited by S. L. Greenslade, 46–247. Louisville: Westminster, 1956.

Anselm, *The Prayers and Meditations of Saint Anselm with the Proslogion.* Translated by Benedicta Ward. London: Penguin Classics, 1973.

Atkinson, Morgan C., ed. *Soul Searching: The Journals of Thomas Merton.* Collegeville, MN: Liturgical, 2008.

Atwood, Craig, D. "The Union of Masculine and Feminine in Zinzendorfian Piety." In *Masculinity, Senses, Spirit,* edited by Katherine M. Faull, 11-37. Lanham, MA: Bucknell University Press, 2011.

Augustine. *The Confessions of Saint Augustine.* Translated by F. J. Sheed. London: Sheed & Ward, 1984.

———. *On the Trinity.* Translated by Arthur West Haddon. Edited by Paul A Boer. Rome: Veritatis Splendor, 2012.

Barry, William. *God and You: Prayer as Personal Relationship.* New York: Paulist, 1987.

Barry, William and Connolly, William. *The Practice of Spiritual Direction.* 2nd ed. New York: Harper One, 2009.

Benedict XVI, Pope. "Pope reflects on God's maternal love." June 8, 2005. http://www.catholicnewsagency.com/news/pope_reflects_on_gods_maternal_love.

Bodo, Murray. *Juniper: Friend of Francis, Fool of God.* Cincinnati: St. Anthony Messenger, 1983.

Bonaventure. *The Soul's Journey into God, The Tree of Life, The Life of Saint Francis.* Mahwah, NJ: Paulist, 1978.

Bos, Johanna. "When You Pray Our Father." *Presbyterian Survey* (May 1981) 12.

Bourgeault, Cynthia and Richard Rohr. *God As Us! The Sacred Feminine & the Sacred Masculine.* Albuquerque, NM: Center for Action and Contemplation, 2011. Compact disc.

Bragan, Kenneth. *The Making of a Saint: A Psychological Study of the Life of Thomas Merton.* Durham, CT: Strategic Book Group, 2011.

Briere, John, N. *Child Abuse Trauma: Theory and Treatment of the Lasting Effects.* London: Sage, 1992.

Brueggemann, Walter. *Genesis.* Atlanta: John Knox, 1982.

Bryant, Christopher. *Jung and the Christian Way.* London: Darton, Longman and Todd, 1983.

Bulkeley, Tim. "The Image of the Invisible God." In *Reconsidering Gender: Evangelical Perspectives,* edited by Myk Habets and Beulah Wood, 20–37. Eugene, OR: Pickwick, 2011.

Burnham, Frederic B., and Charles S. McCoy. *Love, The Foundation of Hope: The Theology of Jurgen Moltmann and Elizabeth Moltmann-Wendel.* San Francisco: Harper & Row, 1988.

Bynum, Caroline. *Jesus as Mother: Studies in the Spirituality of the High Middle Ages.* Berkeley: University of California, 1982.

Carr, David M. *The Erotic Word: Sexuality, Spirituality, and the Bible.* New York: Oxford University Press, 2003.

Clement. ""The Second Epistle of Clement," In *The Ante-Nicene Fathers, Vol.* 7, edited by Philip Schaff, 419-30. North Charleston, SC: CreateSpace, 2017.

The Cloud of Unknowing and the Book of Privy Counseling. Translated by William Johnston. New York: Image, 1973.

Cornwall, Susannah. *Theology and Sexuality.* Norwich, UK: SCM, 2013.

Cozzens, Donald, B. *The Changing Face of the Priesthood: A Reflection on the Priest's Crisis of Soul.* Collegeville, MN: Liturgical, 2000.

Dearborn, Kerry. *Baptized Imagination: The Theology of George MacDonald.* Aldershot, UK: Ashgate, 2006.

Donne, John. *Devotions upon Emergent Occasions.* Ann Arbor: University of Michigan Press, 1959.

———. *Holy Sonnets.* Newton, NJ: Vicarage Hill, 2014.

———. *The Works of John Donne,* vol 5. London: John W. Parker, 1834.

Dorsett, Bob. *Journey to a Woman's Heart.* O'Brien, OR: Bob Dorsett, 2000.

Elie, Paul. *The Life You Save May Be Your Own: An American Pilgrimage.* New York: Farrar, Straus and Giroux, 2003.

Engelsman, Joan C. *The Feminine Dimension of the Divine.* Philadelphia: Westminster, 1979.

Ephrem. *Ephrem the Syrian: Hymns.* Translated by Kathleen E. McVey. Mahwah, NJ: Paulist, 1989.

Eugenio, Damiana L. *Philippine Folk Literature: The Legends.* Manila: University of the Philippines, 1996.

Faull, Katherine M. "Temporal Men and the Eternal Bridegroom: Moravian Masculinity in the Eighteenth Century." In *Masculinity, Senses, Spirit,* 55-80. Lanham, MA: Bucknell University Press, 2011.

Forest, Jim. *Living with Wisdom: A Life of Thomas Merton.* Maryknoll, NY: Orbis, 1991.

Furlong, Monica. *Merton: A Biography.* London: Darton, Longman and Todd, 1985.

Gately, Edwina and Robert Lantz. *Christ in the Margins.* Maryknoll, NY: Orbis, 2003.

Goethe, Johann W. V. *Faust (Part Two).* Translated by Philip Wayne. London: Penguin Classics, 1959.

Goldingay, John. *Approaches to Old Testament Interpretation.* Jacksonville, FL: Clements, 2002.

———. *Key Questions about Biblical Interpretation: Old Testament Answers.* Grand Rapids: Baker Academic, 2011.

———. *Old Testament Theology: Israel's Gospel.* Downers Grove, IL: InterVarsity Press, 2003.

————. *Psalms.* Grand Rapids: Baker Academic, 2008.

Goldingay, Kathleen Scott. "Song of Songs: Lady Wisdom's Riddle Concerning Solomon and his Foreign Wives." Paper presented at Society for Biblical Languages, Vienna, 2014. www.academia.edu/10363687/Lady_Wisdoms-Song_for_Solomon.

Griffin, John Howard. *Follow the Ecstasy: The Hermitage Years of Thomas Merton, 1965–1968.* Maryknoll, NY: Orbis, 1993.

Harvey, Susan A. "Female Imagery for the Divine: The Holy Spirit, the Odes of Solomon, and Early Syriac Tradition." *St. Vladimir's Theological Quarterly* 37, 2/3 (1993) 111–39.

Newman, Barbara. *Sister of Wisdom: St Hildegard's Theology of the Feminine.* Berkeley: University of California Press, 1987.

The Inclusive Bible. New York: Sheed & Ward, 2007.

Irenaeus. *Against Heresies.* Translated by John Keble, London: Aeterna, 2016.

Jewett, Paul, K. *The Ordination of Women: An Essay on the Office of Christian Ministry.* Grand Rapids: Eerdmans, 1980.

John of the Cross. *Collected Works of St. John of the Cross.* Revised edition. Translated by Kavanagh, Kieran and Otilio Rodriguez. Washington, DC: Institute of Carmelite Studies, 1991.

Johnson, Elizabeth A. *She Who Is: The Mystery of God in Feminist Theological Discourse.* 2nd ed. New York: Crossroad, 2002.

————. *Women, Earth, and Creator Spirit.* Notre Dame, IN: Saint Mary's College, 1993.

Johnson, Robert A. *He: Understanding Masculine Psychology.* New York: Harper and Row, 1989.

————. *Inner Gold: Understanding Psychological Projection.* Kihei, HI: Koa Books, 2008.

————. *Inner Work: Using Dreams and Active Imagination for Personal Growth.* New York: Harper and Row, 2009.

————. Interview by Lila Forest. *In Context,* 16 (Spring 1987) 19.

————. *She: Understanding Feminine Psychology.* New York: Harper and Row, 1989.

————. *We: Understanding the Psychology of Romantic Love,* New York: HarperCollins, 1983.

Jung, Carl G. *Answer to Job.* Translated by R. F. C. Hull. London: Routledge, 2012.

————. *The Collected Works of C. G. Jung, Vol. 9: Archetypes and the Collective Unconscious.* 2nd Edition. Translated by R. F. C. Hull. London: Routledge & Kegan Paul, 1969.

————. *Aspects of the Feminine.* Translated by R. F. C. Hull. London: Routledge & Kegan Paul, 1982.

————. *Man and his Symbols.* New York: Dell, 1964.

————. *Memories, Dreams and Reflections.* London, Collins, 1977.

————. *Symbols of Transformation.* Translated by R. F. C. Hull. Princeton: Princeton University Press, 1967.

————. *The Practice of Psychotherapy.* 2d ed. New York: Bollingen, 1966.

Jung, Carl, G. and Sonu Shamdasani. *The Red Book: A Reader's Edition.* New York: Norton, 2009.

Julian of Norwich. *Revelations of Divine Love.* Translated by Clifton Wolters. London: Penguin Classics, 1966.

————. *Showings.* Translated by Edmund Colledge and James Walsh. New York: Paulist, 1978.

Justin Martyr. "Dialogue with Trypho." In *Saint Justin Martyr, The Fathers of the Church: A New Translation*, vol. 6, translated by Thomas B. Falls, 141-365. Washington, DC: Catholic University of America, 1948.

Kohler, Kaufmann and Ludwig Blau. "Shekinah." *Jewish Encyclopedia*. http://www. jewishencyclopedia.com/articles/13537-shekinah.

Kramp, Joseph, M. "Merton's Melancholia: Margie, Monasticism, and the Religion of Hope." *Pastoral Psychology* 54 (2007) 441–58.

Kruger, Baxter C. *The Shack Revisited*. New York: Faith Words, 2012.

Lewis, C. S. *George MacDonald: An Anthology*. London: Geoffrey Bles, 1946.

———. *The Problem of Pain*. San Francisco: Harper, 2001.

McCaslin, Susan. "Merton and Hagia Sophia." In *Merton and Hesychasm, Prayer of the Heart,* edited by Berndette Dieker and Jonathon Montaldo, 235–54. Louisville, KY: Fons Vitae, 2003.

MacDonald, George. *At the Back of the North Wind*. Uhrichsville, OH: Barbour, 2005.

———. *A Dish of Orts*. London: S. Low, Marston, 1880. http://www.gutenberg.org/ files/9393/9393-h/9393-h.htm.

———. "The Fantastic Imagination." In *A Dish of Orts: Chiefly Papers on the Imagination and on Shakespeare,* 313–22. London: S. Low, Marston, 1893.

———. *A Hidden Life and Other Poems*. London: Longman, 1864.

———. *Lilith: A Romance*. New York: Dover, 2008.

———. *Phantastes*. London: Paternoster, 2008.

———. *The Wise Woman: A Parable*. London: Strahan, 1875.

Matheson, Lister M., ed. *Icons of the Middle Ages: Rulers, Writer, Rebels, and Saints*, vol 1. Santa Barbara, CA: Greenwood, 2012.

McFague, Sallie. *Models of God: Theology for an Ecological, Nuclear Age*. Minneapolis: Fortress, 1987.

Mendelson, Michael. "George MacDonald's *Lilith* and Conventions of Ascent." *Studies in Scottish Literature* 20, no. 1 (1985) 208. http://scholarcommons.sc.edu/cgi/ viewcontent.cgi?article=1153&context=ssl.

Merton, Thomas. *Basic Principles of Monastic Spirituality*. Bardstown, KY: Abbey of Our Lady of Gethsemani, 1957.

———. *Dancing in the Water of Life: The Journals of Thomas Merton, 1963–1965*, vol. 5. Edited by Robert E. Daggy. New York: HarperCollins, 1997.

———. *Elected Silence: The Autobiography of Thomas Merton*. London: Hollis and Carter, 1950.

———. "Hagia Sophia." In *In the Dark before Dawn: New Selected Poems of Thomas Merton*, edited by Lynn R. Szabo, 65–71. New York: New Directions, 2005.

———. *The Intimate Merton: His Life from his Journals*. San Francisco: HarperCollins, 1999.

———. *Learning to Love: Exploring Solitude and Freedom*. Edited by Christine M. Bochen. New York: HarperSanFransisco, 1997.

———. *A Life in Letters: The Essential Collection*. New York: Harper One, 2008.

———. "Mid Summer Diary." In *Learning to Love: Exploring Solitude and Freedom*, edited by Christine M. Bochen, 300–348. New York: HarperSanFransisco, 1997.

———. *New Seeds of Contemplation*. New York: New Directions, 2007.

———. *A Search for Solitude: Pursuing the Monk's True Life*. New York: HarperSanFrancisco, 1996.

———. *The Seven Storey Mountain*, New York: Harcourt Brace, 1948.

———. *The Sign of Jonas*. New York: Harvest, 1953.

Mollenkott, Virginia. *The Divine Feminine: The Biblical Imagery of God as Female*. New York: Crossroads, 1988.

Nelson, James B. *The Intimate Connection: Male Sexuality, Masculine Spirituality*. Philadelphia: Westminster, 1988.

Nettelhorst, Robin P. "More than just a Controversy: All about the Holy Spirit." *Quartz Hill School of Theology Journal*. www.theology.edu/journal/volume3/spirit.htm.

Neuhouser, David. "God as *Mother* in George MacDonald's 'The Wise Woman.'" *Christianity and the Arts* 4.4 (2000) 42–44.

Nouwen, Henri J. M. *Life of the Beloved: Spiritual Living in a Secular World*. New York: Crossroad, 1992.

Origen. *On First Principles*, 2.6.2. Translated by G. W. Butterworth. New York: Harper and Row, 1966.

———. *The Song of Songs: Commentary and Homilies*. Translated by R. P. Lawson. Westminster, MD: Newman, 1957.

Page, Nick. "Introduction," in *Phantastes* by George MacDonald, 7–30. London: Paternoster, 2008.

Peck, M. Scott. *People of the Lie*. New York: Simon and Schuster, 1983.

Pius XII, Pope. "Apostolic Constitution Munificentissimus Deus Defining the Dogma of the Assumption." http://w2.vatican.va/content/pius-xii/en/post_constitutions/documents/hf_p-xii_apc_19501101_munificentissimus-deus.html.

Pramuk, Christopher. *Sophia: The Hidden Christ of Thomas Merton*. Collegeville, MN: Liturgical Press, 2009.

Raeper, William. *George MacDonald*. Tring, UK: Lion, 1987.

Ramachandran, V. S. and E. M. Hubbard. "Hearing Colors, Tasting Shapes." *Scientific American* 288, no. 5 (May 2003) 42–50.

Ringma, Charles. *Hear the Ancient Wisdom*. Eugene, OR: Cascade, 2013.

Rizzuto, Ana. *The Birth of the Living God: A Psychoanalytic Study*. Chicago: University of Chicago Press, 1981.

Robinson, James, "James Robinson and the Shack." *My Soul Pants for God & God Alone!* July 21, 2008. http://soulpants.wordpress.com/2008/07/21/james-robinson-and-the-shack.

Rohr, Richard. *Adam's Return: The Five Promises of Male Initiation*. New York: Crossroad, 2004.

———. *From Wild Man to Wise Man: Reflections on Male Spirituality*. Cincinnati: St. Anthony Messenger, 2005.

———. *The Gates of the Temple: Sexuality and Spirituality* . Albuquerque, NM: Center for Action and Contemplation, 2005. Compact disc.

———. *Immortal Diamond*. San Francisco: Jossey-Bass, 2013.

———. *Unitive Consciousness: Beyond Gender*. Cincinnati: Franciscan Media, 2012.

Rohr, Richard and Joseph Martos. *The Wild Man's Journey: Reflections on Male Spirituality*. Cincinnati: St. Anthony Messenger Press, 1996.

Rolheiser, Ronald. *The Holy Longing: The Search for a Christian Spirituality*. New York: Image, 2014.

———. *Seeking Spirituality*. London: Hodder and Stoughton, 1998.

Ruether, Rosemary Radford. *Mary—The Feminine Face of the Church*. London: SCM Press, 1979.

Schillebeeckx, E. *Mary, Mother of the Redemption*. Translated by N. D. Smith. London: Sheed and Ward, 1964.

Schneiders, Sandra M. *Women and the Word: The Gender of God in the New Testament and the Spirituality of Women*. New York: Paulist, 1986.

Scofield, Cyrus, I. *Bibletools*. http://bibletools.org/index.cfm/fuseaction/Bible.show/sVerseID/399/eVerseID/399/RTD/SCO.

Shamdasani, Sonu. "Introduction" in *The Red Book: A Reader's Edition*, 1–95. New York: Norton, 2009.

Shaw, Mark. *Beneath the Mask of Holiness: Thomas Merton and the Forbidden Love Affair that Set him Free*. New York: Palgrave Macmillan, 2009.

"The Shepherd of Hermas." Translated by J. B. Lightfoot. http://www.earlychristianwritings.com/text/shepherd-lightfoot.html.

Snead, Holly M. *The Holy Days of God, the Holidays of Man*. Bloomington, IN: iUniverse, 2012.

Stramara, Daniel, F. *Praying—with the Saints—to God our Mother*. Eugene, OR: Cascade, 2012.

Swidler, Leonard. *Biblical Affirmations of Woman*. Philadelphia: Westminster John Knox, 1979.

Trible, Phyllis. *God and the Rhetoric of Sexuality*. Minneapolis: Fortress Press, 1978.

Vanier, Jean. *Drawn into the Mystery of Jesus through the Gospel of John*. New York: Paulist, 2004.

Waldron, Robert, G. *The Wounded Heart of Thomas Merton*. Mahwah, NJ: Paulist, 2012.

Williams, Rowan. "The Body's Grace." In *Theology and Sexuality: Classic and Contemporary Readings*, edited by Eugene F. Rogers, 309–21. Oxford: Blackwell, 2002.

Young, W. Paul. *Cross Roads*. New York: Faith Words, 2012.

———. *Eve*. New York: Simon and Schuster, 2015.

———. *The Shack*. Newbury Park, CA: Windblown, 2007.

———. "Wm. Paul Young—About." Author website. http://wmpaulyoung.com/wm-paul-young-about/.

Zuercher, Suzanne. *The Ground of Love and Truth: Reflections on Thomas Merton's Relationship with a Woman Known as "M."* Chicago: In Extenso, 2014.

Scripture Index

Scripture Index

Name Index

11574634R00092

Printed in Germany
by Amazon Distribution
GmbH, Leipzig